AIR TOOLS
HOW TO CHOOSE, USE AND MAINTAIN THEM

RICK PETERS

Sterling Publishing Co., Inc.
New York

Acknowledgements

Butterick Media Production Staff

Design: Triad Design Group, Ltd.
Cover Design: Elizabeth Berry
Photography: Christopher Vendetta
Illustrations: Greg Kopfer, Triad Design

Assoc. Art Director: Monica Gaige-Rosensweig
Copy Editor: Barbara Webb
Page Layout: David Joinnides
Index: Nan Badgett
Assoc. Managing Editor: Stephanie Marracco
Project Director: Caroline Politi
President: Art Joinnides

Special thanks to Bob Skummer of Jet Equipment and Tools, Inc. for supplying product and technical information, the folks at Duofast for supplying air nailers and technical information, and Hankison International for providing the drawings of membrane dryers on page 23. Thanks to the production staff at Butterick Media for their continuing support. And finally, a heartfelt thanks to my constant inspiration: Cheryl, Lynne, Will and Beth. R.P.

Every effort has been made to ensure that all the information in this book is accurate. However, due to differing conditions, tools and individual skill, the publisher cannot be responsible for any injuries, losses, or other damages which may result from the use of information in this book.

3 3113 01950 9969

Library of Congress Cataloging-in-Publication Data

Peters, Rick
    Air Tools: how to choose, use, and maintain them/Rick Peters
        p.   cm.
ISBN 0-8069-3692-4
    1. Power tools.   I. Title.
TJ1195.P43 2000
621.9'04--dc21   99-086643

ISBN 0-8069-3692-4

Published by Sterling Publishing Company, Inc.
387 Park Avenue South, New York, N.Y. 10016
©2000, Butterick Company, Inc., Rick Peters
Distributed in Canada by Sterling Publishing, c/o Canadian Manda Group, One Atlantic Avenue, Suite 105, Toronto, Ontario, Canada M6K 3E7
Distributed in Great Britain and Europe by Cassell PLC, Wellington House, 125 Strand, London WC2R 0BB, England
Distributed in Australia by Capricorn Link (Australia) Pty. Ltd., P.O. Box 6651, Baulkham Hills, Business Centre, NSW 2153, Australia

Printed in the United States of America
All rights reserved

B
THE BUTTERICK© PUBLISHING COMPANY
161 Avenue of the Americas
New York, N.Y. 10013

INTRODUCTION

I've been using air-powered tools in my shop for years. Often when a woodworking or home improvement enthusiast neighbor stops by they'll ask "Why would you want to use an air-powered tool instead of an electric tool?" Here's what I tell them.

- Air tools are lightweight: Since air tools are powered by a compressor, they don't need motors. This means they typically weigh less than their electric cousins.

- Air tools are compact: No internal motor also means air tools can be smaller and more compact. The average air-powered drill is half the size of an electric drill. It fits better in your hand and is more comfortable to use.

- Air tools are powerful: Although compact and small, air tools are just as powerful as the electric equivalent. A bonus, the air that flows through the tool to power it also cools it down. Unlike an electric tool that heats up the harder you work it, an air tool stays cool and won't bog down.

- Air tools are precise: Soon after I started working with air tools, I discovered that they could add precision to my work. An example of this is putting up crown molding. Instead of hammering in nails and occasionally denting the molding, a finish nailer will drive and set a nail in a blink of an eye with nary a dent.

- Air tools are quiet: Although air tools make some noise when used, they certainly don't emit that high-pitched "nails-on-chalkboard" whine that electric motors produce. This is particularly noticeable when you compare electric and air-powered sanders.

- Air tools are convenient: Wouldn't it be convenient if all your electric tools used a single power cord that was detachable? This way all you'd have to do is plug in one cord and then hook it up to the tool you wanted to use. No more jumble of cords. That's exactly how it is with air tools. They're all powered by and accept the same single air hose.

- Air tools speed up tedious work: From pressure-washing the deck to removing old paint with a sandblaster, there's an air-powered tool to help speed up virtually any tedious chore. An air nailer or spray gun can easily cut framing or painting work time in half.

The only problem I've discovered with air-powered tools is there isn't any decent information on them available—like what to look for when you're interested in buying one, or how to use them, and what to do if things go wrong. The tool manuals aren't much help: The first half is warnings, the second half is in another language.

In this book, I'll start by describing what to look for when you go to purchase the power plant for air tools—the compressor. Chapter 1 looks at oil-lubricated and oil-less compressors and identifies what features are important, differences in construction, and issues like portability and cost. At the end of the chapter, there's a decision-making flowchart to help you wade through the options.

In Chapter 2, I'll take you through the myriad accessories available for your compressor. From the essential setup components like filters, regulators, and air hoses to the individual tools like spray guns, sanders, drills, and air nailers. Here again, I've included a couple of decision-making flowcharts to help make your tool buying easier.

Basic operations are covered in Chapter 3, starting with how to set up your air system, whether it's portable or permanent. Then on to sandblasting, pressure washing, and using a sander, impact wrenches, and die grinders.

Chapter 4 looks at two of the more advanced operations: spraying on paint and finishes and using air nailers. Of all air-powered tools, air nailers need carefulest handling. That's why I've included a special section in this chapter on fastening safety.

I've provided detailed drawings and building instructions for several of my favorite shop-made jigs for air tools in Chapter 5, from advanced jigs like a wall-mounted air station to a simple hose caddy for a portable compressor.

Maintenance and repair is what Chapter 6 is all about. Daily, weekly, and monthly maintenance suggestions to keep you compressor running smooth. When a problem does arrive, there's information on repairing and rebuilding a compressor. I've also included suggested maintenance and repair instructions for two of the harder-working air tools: spray guns and air nailers.

The last chapter, Chapter 7, describes common problems you're likely to encounter when using air-powered tools, and their solutions.

All in all, this makes for a comprehensive guide that will help you choose, use, and maintain air tools. Armed with this information, I hope that you'll reach for air tools with greater confidence to handle a wide variety of jobs around the home and shop.

Rick Peters
Spring 2000

CHAPTER 1
SELECTING AN AIR COMPRESSOR

I started using air tools well over 20 years ago, when I was in the service—mainly pressure washers and simple air nozzles to clean parts. Even then, I realized that you could get a lot of work done with compressed air. Since then, I've used hundreds of air tools hooked up to dozens of compressors to do everything from building walls with air nailers to cutting custom profiles on shaper knives with a die grinder.

The main reason air tools have become so popular recently is that more and more people have discovered that they combine power and precision with efficiency. But using air to power tools has other advantages.

First, since air continuously flows through the tool, there's less chance for heat to build up— which means longer tool life. Second, the majority of air-powered tools run more quietly than their electric cousins. And third, air-powered tools generally weigh less, since they don't have the added weight of an electric motor. All together this means a cooler, lighter tool that's less fatiguing to use and easier to handle.

Although compressors and air tools have been used for decades in the automotive and manufacturing industries, they've gained widespread acceptance only recently. With the advent of the nail gun, air-powered nailers have quickly replaced the hammer in the construction trades. Now it's not uncommon to find a compressor in a workshop providing power to nail guns, staplers, pressure washers, spray guns, sanders, impact wrenches, drills,...the list goes on.

In this chapter, I'll cover the power source for all air tools—the compressor. In order to wade through the many compressors out there, I start by defining the two major types: oil-lubricated and oil-less (*pages 7–9*). Then on to what features to look for when you begin shopping for an air compressor: horsepower and operating voltage (*page 10*), tank size (*page 11*), type of construction (*page 12*), and finally portability (*pages 14–15*).

I conclude the chapter with cost charts, recommendations, and a decision-making flowchart to help you select the perfect compressor to match your needs (*pages 16–17*).

Although compressors can be powered by either gas or electricity, the majority of compressors are electric. Gas compressors require constant attention—changing the oil, adding gas—it's like having another vehicle. The only reason I see to buy a gas compressor is when there's no access to electricity. Otherwise, you're better off sticking with an electric version. That's why in this chapter I've concentrated solely on electric compressors.

There are two types of electric compressor: oil-lubricated (*above left*) and oil-less (*above right*). Oil-lubricated compressors need regular maintenance: Oil must be

checked and topped off, and the filter and oil will need to be replaced periodically. Despite this, they have a reputation for hardiness and dependability on the job site. They will often run twice as long as oil-less compressors between rebuilds. A typical well-designed oil-lubricated compressor will need a rebuild after 2,000 hours of use—that's 3 to 4 years if you use your compressor 10 hours a week.

Oil-less, oil-free, or "self-lubricated" compressors run without oil. Instead, they use nonmetal piston rings, Teflon-coated parts, and sealed bearings. In effect, they are maintenance-free—but

only for a while. Since they don't use a lubricant, internal parts are constantly rubbing against each other. Even with friction-reducing parts, this type of compressor will need a rebuild roughly twice as often as an oil-lubricated compressor.

If you visited a bunch of construction sites, you'd find that most contractors stick with an oil-lubricated compressor. With the way they work a compressor, they've found that they just don't get the life out of an oil-less compressor that they do out of a lubricated compressor. The general feeling is, it's a lot cheaper to buy oil than a new compressor.

OIL-LUBRICATED COMPRESSORS

Oil-lubricated compressors are simple, efficient, often compact, and available in one- or two-stage versions. A single-stage compressor squeezes air in a single piston stroke to 25 to 125 pounds per square inch (psi). In a two-stage compressor, intermediate pressurized air is further compressed in a second cylinder to 100 to 250 psi.

Since most air tools require only 90 psi to operate, a single-stage compressor will handle just about any job. Also, two-stage compressors are more expensive and heavier than single-stage versions and typically require 220 volts to operate (*see page 12 for more on this*).

The typical oil-lubricated compressor (*see the drawing below*) consists of an air pump powered by either a gas engine or an electric motor, a tank to store the compressed air, and handles and/or wheels to make the compressor portable.

There's also an air outlet to tap into the tank, petcocks or drains to empty condensed water from the tank, and usually a built-in regulator and pressure gauge to adjust and monitor airflow.

It's important to note that oil-lubricated compressors are splash-lubricated. This means that they must be run on a level surface. If the compressor is set up on a slope, the crankshaft won't splash enough oil onto the internal parts, resulting in accelerated wear and eventual failure.

ANATOMY OF AN OIL-LUBRICATED COMPRESSOR

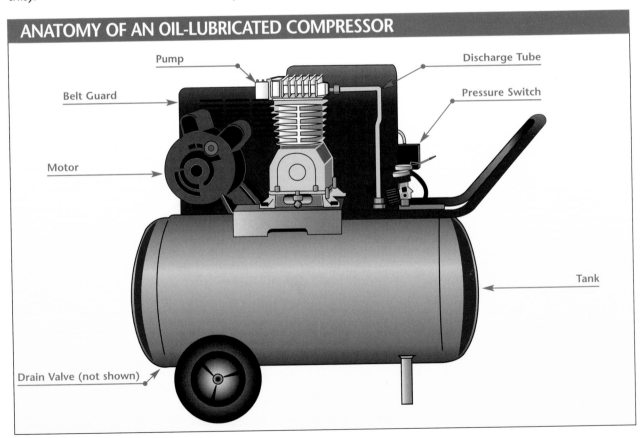

Pump

Belt Guard

Motor

Discharge Tube

Pressure Switch

Tank

Drain Valve (not shown)

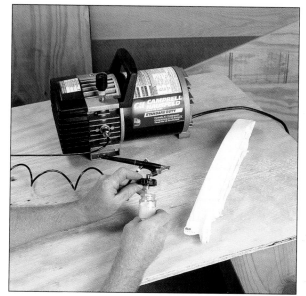

Oil-less compressors use non-metal piston rings and Teflon-coated parts in lieu of oil to keep the internal parts running smoothly. Without a lubricant, however, the internal parts are constantly rubbing against each other. Because of this, oil-less compressors have a tendency to be loud, sometimes really loud. I made the mistake once of leaving an oil-less compressor ON down in my basement. When the pressure dropped off sometime in the middle of the night and the compressor kicked on, I was sure we were under attack.

On the plus side, since there's no oil to splash around for lubrication, you don't have to worry about keeping an oil-less compressor level—it can be used at almost any angle. Also, since there's no oil inside the air pump, no oil can get into the air line to contaminate finishes (unless you're intentionally adding it via a lubricator; *see page 22*).

Similar to an oil-lubricated compressor, an oil-less compressor (*see drawing below*) has an air pump powered by an electric motor, a tank to store the compressed air, and handles and/or wheels to make the compressor portable. It also has an air outlet to tap into the tank, petcocks or drains to empty condensed water from the tank, and usually a built-in regulator and pressure gauge to adjust and monitor the airflow.

ANATOMY OF AN OIL-LESS COMPRESSOR

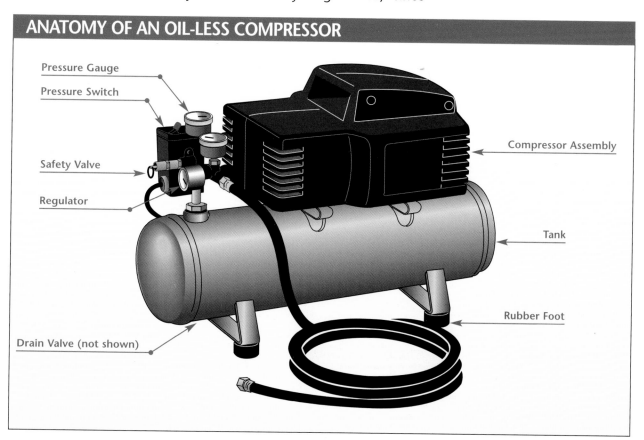

Pressure Gauge

Pressure Switch

Safety Valve

Regulator

Compressor Assembly

Tank

Rubber Foot

Drain Valve (not shown)

FEATURES OF COMPRESSORS

Although air compressors are typically rated by horsepower—varying anywhere from ½ hp to 10 hp and up—what's really important is the volume of air they are capable of producing at a sustained pressure. The secret to selecting a compressor is defining what air tools you'll be using (now and in the future). As long as you find a compressor that can produce the volume of air you need for these tools, the horsepower is insignificant.

Most air tools run at 90 psi (pounds per square inch)—a pressure that virtually every compressor is capable of producing. The catch is identifying what volume of air (at 90 psi) each tool needs to operate smoothly and efficiently. (Volume of airflow is measured in cfm, or cubic feet per minute.)

All air tools have varying cfm needs; see the cfm chart *below left* for typical cfm ratings of common tools. For instance, a narrow crown stapler used intermittently will need only 1 to 3 cfm. On the other hand, a random-orbit sander when run continuously will gulp 6 to 10 cubic feet of air per minute.

Since most compressors are rated for a 50% duty cycle (half on, half off), running a tool like a random-orbit sander continuously will cause the compressor to run more often—possibly continuously. To get around this, you'll need a compressor that produces a cfm higher than the highest rated tool you're planning on using; see the chart *below right* for typical cfm production of various compressors. Note: If you're planning to run multiple tools simultaneously, you'll need to add up the cfm requirements of the individual tools.

Although it may sound like a good idea when a compressor salesman suggests doubling the highest-cfm-rated tool you're planning on using to identify the maximum cfm rating for your dream compressor, it may not be. Since many air tools require 4 to 6 cfm, the majority of the compressors on the market that can produce double this (8 to 12 cfm) require 220 volts to operate—which may not be readily accessible in your shop or home.

If you do find a high-cfm compressor that's designed to run on 110 volts, it'll most certainly pop breakers every time it kicks on. (As a general rule of thumb, compressors rated 5-hp and above require 220 volts.)

TYPICAL CFM RATINGS

Tool	CFM	PSI
⅜" drill	4–6	70–90
⅜" impact wrench	3–6	70–90
Stapler	1–3	70–90
Brad nailer	2–4	70–90
Finish nailer	4–7	70–90
Framing nailer	4–10	70–90
Coil nailer	5–9	70–90
Pressure washer	3–5	70–90
Sandblast gun	2–3	30–90
Random-orbit sander	6–10	70–90
Jitterbug sander	5–9	70–90
In-line sander	5–9	70–90
Screwdriver	2–6	70–90
Air brush	1–2	25–40
Paint sprayer	1–5	10–70

TYPICAL CFM PRODUCTION

Compressor Type	CFM at 90 PSI
Tankless	1–2
Hand-carried	2–4
Medium-duty	3–5
Heavy-duty	5–10

No-tank One of the tank configurations you can choose is no tank at all. Small oil-less compressors are available sans tank; but they run continuously and are hard-pressed to deliver the kind of air volume you'll need. They're best suited for light jobs like inflating pool toys and sports equipment and for powering low-cfm tools like an airbrush.

Without a tank for storage, this type of compressor runs continuously; this means any air tool you hook up must be of the "bleeder" variety; that is, it safely shunts off any air it doesn't need to operate.

Small and medium tank(s) Small and medium-sized tanks are available in two common configurations: pancake and twin-tank. Small tanks, like the pancake version shown, typically hold 1 to 4 gallons. Medium-sized tanks often consist of "twin" tanks; the tanks can be stacked vertically or horizontally.

Medium tanks hold anywhere from 4 to 12 gallons. I prefer twin tanks for portables because you can carry the compressor with the tanks against your leg. Since a compressor gets hot with use, carrying it like this can prevent accidental burns.

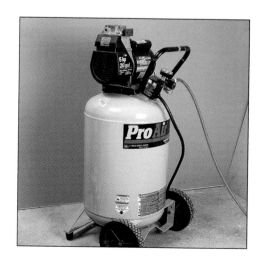

Large tank The larger the tank, the longer you can work at a desired pressure and flow rate—but at the cost of portability. Large compressors like the one shown often have single tanks that store 10 to 60 gallons.

One reason many large compressors use a single tank is for balance. A single tank centered on the compressor helps make these quite heavy tools a bit easier to move around. A word of caution: The size of the tank does not reflect the ability of the compressor to produce air.

Air Tools

Single and two-stage compressors

I think that one of the most confusing things to come across when sorting through the myriad compressors is to find two compressors with the same horsepower rating but producing widely different airflows. This often has to do with the design of the compressor: whether it's single or two-stage, or whether it has one or more pistons.

A single-stage compressor (*top drawing*) squeezes air in a single piston stroke to 25 to 125 psi. In a two-stage compressor (*bottom drawing*), intermediate pressurized air is further compressed in a second cylinder to 100 to 250 psi. Since most air tools require only 90 to 100 psi to operate, a single-stage compressor will handle just about any job you can throw at it. Also, two-stage compressors tend to be more expensive and heavier than single-stage units and usually require 220 volts.

In between single and two-stage compressors are double reciprocating compressors. Although this type of compressor sports twin pistons, they're still one-stage compressors, as they compress air in a single piston stroke. But with two cylinders, they squeeze twice as much air, resulting in double the air delivery.

A compressor basically works on the same principle as a bicycle tire pump. When a piston inside a cylinder is drawn back, it pulls air into the chamber. When the cylinder pushes forward, it compresses the air. The only difference with a compressor is the piston is powered by a gas or electric motor via a crankshaft and the air is stored in a tank. The motor runs until a certain pressure is achieved in the tank (typically 110 to 120 psi), and then it automatically shuts off. A predetermined dip in pressure (usually around 80 to 90 psi) reactivates the cycle.

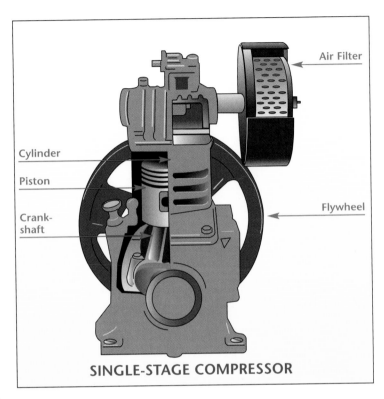

Air Filter

Cylinder

Piston

Crank-shaft

Flywheel

SINGLE-STAGE COMPRESSOR

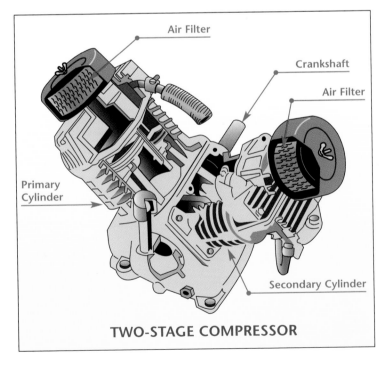

Air Filter

Crankshaft

Air Filter

Primary Cylinder

Secondary Cylinder

TWO-STAGE COMPRESSOR

Filters: foam vs. felt One of the things I look for when buying a compressor is what type of air filter it uses. The two most common filters are foam (*left*) and felt (*right*).

I've always preferred foam filters because they are really easy to clean and reuse. Just wash them in kerosene or liquid detergent. When dry, saturate with engine oil, squeeze out the excess, and reinstall. I've never had much luck cleaning felt filters and usually end up buying a new one when the old one gets clogged.

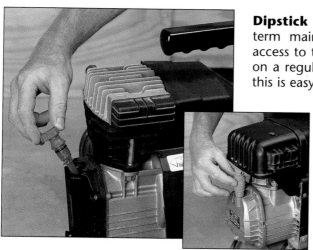

Dipstick location Another thing I look for regarding long-term maintenance on an oil-lubricated compressor is easy access to the oil dipstick. Since you'll be checking the oil level on a regular basis, it makes sense to find a compressor where this is easy to do.

The compressor shown has a readily accessible dipstick with clear markings. The dipstick in the compressor shown in the inset is so poorly located that you have to either bend it or remove the air filter to lift the dipstick out.

Drain type and location In addition to good access to the dipstick, it's important that the tank drain(s) be easy to reach. Draining condensed water out of the tank is a daily chore. Here again, you should look for drains or petcocks that are both well located and easy to use.

The tank drain in the photo is a good example of thoughtful design—from the location to the large turnbuckle. The poor location of the drain shown in the inset forces the user to virtually lay the tank on its face to drain it.

PORTABILITY

Weight What is "portable?" When I was in the service, the general rule was, "Paint it gray and put a handle on it." To this day, my back shudders at the thought of some of the "portable" gear I lugged around. To me, weight is a big deal. Even if wheels are involved, you still have to overcome gravity.

If you're looking for a truly portable compressor, go to a home center or tool warehouse and pick up each portable and walk around the store. You'll quickly find out which style works best for you.

Wheels Another misconception regarding portability is, "It's got wheels, so it must be portable." True, wheels can make even a heavy compressor easier to move around—but they must be of proper size and be located correctly.

As for wheel size, the bigger the better. The large-diameter wheels on the left compressor shown will navigate potholes, curbs, steps, and most obstructions with ease. The small wheels on the compressor on the right will catch on almost anything—a scrap of lumber, even an extension cord.

Balance Even with reasonable weight and a good set of wheels, not all portable compressors are easy to maneuver. This has to do with the balance of the compressor itself, along with the number of wheels. It was nerve-racking to roll the single-wheel compressor shown up a ramp into a truck.

A dual-wheel compressor with wheels spread comfortably apart would have been better. If you do decide to go with a single-wheel compressor, make sure to give it a spin in the parking lot to test its balance.

Tank location The location of the tank or tanks on a portable compressor will also have an impact on how easy it is to move around. This is especially true for small compressors without wheels. Pancake-style compressors typically have the tank centered below the engine for good balance.

Twin tank designs (like the one shown) with tanks that are stacked vertically have pluses and minuses. Having lighter tanks on one side means the compressor will tip when you pick it up. On the plus side, you can carry it with the tanks against your leg and prevent burns from a hot compressor.

Handles The location, size, and length of the compressor's handles are the final thing to consider when looking for a portable machine. Here again, the best way to ferret out the best for you is to try out the various compressors available.

The compressor shown has dual grips that are quite comfortable. The only problem I had was that the handles were too short for me and I had to stoop over whenever I rolled it around—pretty uncomfortable. But for a shorter person, the handle length may be just right. You'll know only if you try it out for yourself.

A COMPRESSOR-LESS TANK?

If you're really looking for the ultimate in portability, consider an auxiliary tank like the one shown here. Without a compressor, a tank like this weighs only a few pounds. Just like a scuba tank, these small tanks are designed to be filled with air, used, and refilled. Their big disadvantage is that they're good only for small jobs (like nailing up a few pieces of trim with a brad nailer) or to power extremely low–cfm-demanding tools (like an airbrush).

COST RANGES

The first thing to ask yourself when shopping for a compressor is what air tools do you plan on using (now and in the future). Although most air tools are designed to run at 90 psi, the volume of air (cfm) that each tool needs to operate varies dramatically.

Identify which tool needs the most air (*see the chart on page 10*), and make sure the compressor you buy can provide at least its minimum cfm rating. If you're planning on using multiple tools simultaneously, you'll need to add up the cfm requirements of the individual tools.

Depending on quality and features, you can pay a little or a lot for a compressor. The chart shown *at right* lists a general price range, along with common features of the four types of compressors that most homeowners would be interested in. This is intended to give you a rough idea of the approximate cost.

Beware when looking at compressors not to be unduly impressed by tank size. It's common with some manufacturers to stick a large tank with a grossly undersized compressor. Check the horsepower and cfm capacity of the compressor, and match it to the general tank size guidelines in the chart *below*.

Although these big tanks will provide sustained airflow once they're full, they have to run a long time to fill the tank so it can come up to pressure. On my mid-sized compressor, I can flip it on and by the time I've pulled out the hose and unpacked and hooked up an air tool, it's ready to go. With one of these "super" tanks, you can go get coffee and come back and it'll still be chugging away, building up pressure.

It's also worth mentioning again here that the higher horsepower/cfm compressors (5-hp and above 5-cfm) will generally require 220 volts to operate. If you encounter a compressor this large that runs on 110 volts, odds are it'll regularly trip the breaker whenever it kicks on.

TYPICAL COST RANGES

Type	Horsepower	Tank Size	Cost Range
Tankless	½–¾	none	$100–$200
Hand-carried	¾–1	1–4 gallons	$150–$300
Medium-duty	1½–2	7–10 gallons	$250–$600
Heavy-duty	3–5	20–60 gallons	$400–$800

RECOMMENDATIONS

If you're planning on using high-cfm tools like framing nailers and random-orbit sanders, I recommend a large compressor (around 3-hp) with a 20- to 30-gallon tank. These will cost anywhere between $400 and $800, depending on quality.

If you won't be working with air-gobbling tools, a small portable compressor (around 1½-hp) with a 4- to 6-gallon tank and a 25-foot hose will do the job. Here again, depending on quality, they'll set you back between $250 and $600.

Regardless of the size, I recommend sticking with an oil-lubricated compressor. If properly maintained, it'll last a lot longer than an oil-less compressor. I also like the fact that if it breaks down, I can tear it apart and fix it. Quite often when an oil-less compressor goes down, it's not repairable (or if it is, it would cost less to buy a new one).

In buying a compressor, I think that a little overkill isn't such a bad thing. Odds are, you'll be happier in the long run if you buy more compressor than you need at the time. I'm not talking about twice the cfm you need, just a couple cfm more. If you can't decide between a 3-cfm and a 4-cfm compressor with similar features, buy the larger one. You'll be glad you did.

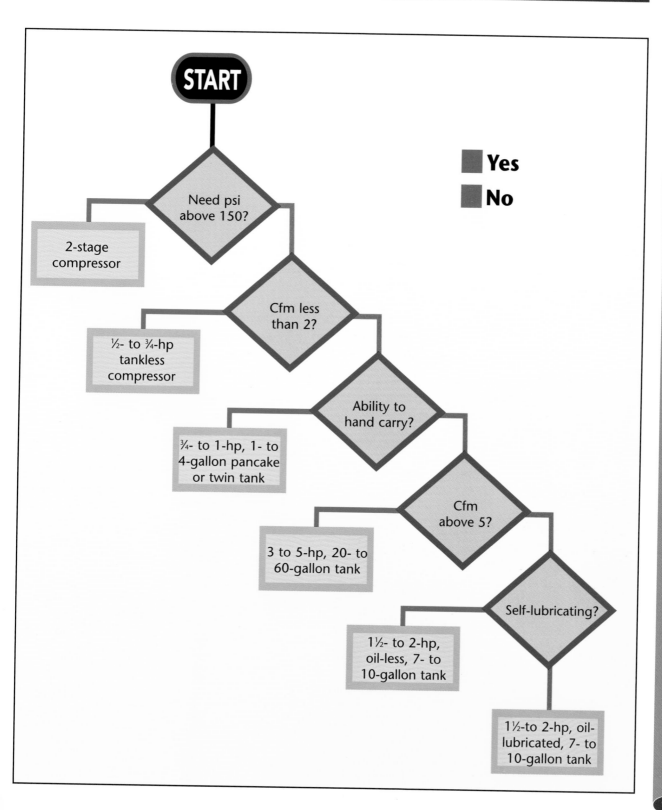

START

Yes
No

Need psi above 150?

2-stage compressor

Cfm less than 2?

½- to ¾-hp tankless compressor

Ability to hand carry?

¾- to 1-hp, 1- to 4-gallon pancake or twin tank

Cfm above 5?

3 to 5-hp, 20- to 60-gallon tank

Self-lubricating?

1½- to 2-hp, oil-less, 7- to 10-gallon tank

1½-to 2-hp, oil-lubricated, 7- to 10-gallon tank

Air Tools

CHAPTER

2 ACCESSORIES

An air compressor without accessories is like a computer without software: It's big and powerful but can't really do anything. And just like accessories for computers, the range of compressor accessories available may seem mind-boggling.

But wading through them all can be simple if you take a systematic approach. The first thing to do is identify what each different accessory can do for you, determine whether you need it, and then compare features versus costs.

In this chapter, I'll start with the must-have accessories that your compressor needs to keep clean air flowing to all of your air tools. In particular, I'll discuss those tools you'll need for a typical setup: a regulator to control pressure, a filter to clean the air, a lubricator to oil your tools automatically, and a dryer if you're planning on doing a lot of spray painting (*pages 19–23*). Then on to the myriad hoses and fittings available (*pages 24–25*).

Next, I'll take you through the many types of spray guns offered by manufacturers to handle an array of materials like paint, stain, clear finishes, even adhesives. Standard and detail spray guns, types of nozzles, feed type, material holders, and airbrushes are covered on pages 26–30.

Sandblasters and pressure washers are gaining in popularity among homeowners—they can really speed up a tedious cleaning or scraping job (*page 31*).

Some of my favorite air tools— sanders, grinders, drills, impact wrenches, staplers, and screwdrivers—are described on pages 32–33.

I've devoted the rest of the chapter to air nailers. That's because of all the air tools out there, the multitude of nailer types and options are almost dizzying. I'll start with the big guns—framing nailers—then on to finish nailers, narrow crown staplers, and finally brad nailers (*pages 34-35, 36-37, 38, and 39, respectively*).

Because of the inherent danger of these tools, there's also a special section on the various safety features available (*pages 40–41*).

To help you make the decision-making process as painless as possible, I've included charts with cost ranges, overall recommendations, and flowcharts (for spray guns and air nailers) on pages 42 and 43.

Armed with this information, you should be able to confidently select the accessories that are best for you. (Now, if you could only find someone else to pay for them all!)

TYPICAL COMPRESSOR SETUP

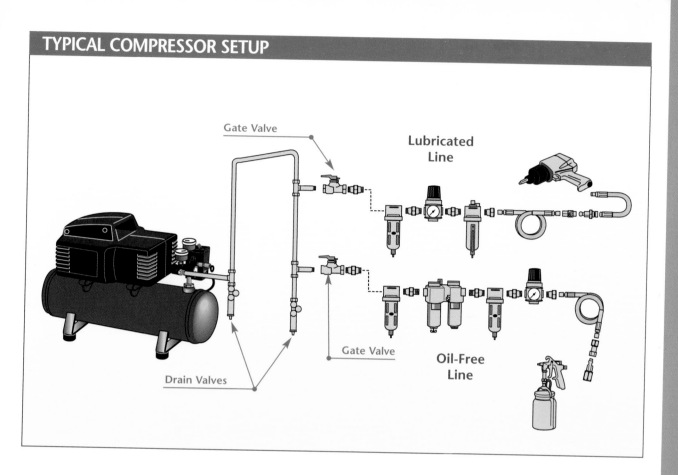

Gate Valve

Lubricated Line

Drain Valves

Gate Valve

Oil-Free Line

Some of the first accessories you should purchase for your compressor are really designed to enhance the performance of your air tools—and protect them from damage.

In particular, you should buy a regulator to control the pressure going to a tool (*page 20*), a filter to provide clean, dry air to the tools (*page 21*), and a lubricator to keep everything running smoothly (*page 22*).

In many cases, you can buy all three of these accessories as a set that comes already assembled. All you have to do is hook up the line from the compressor to the intake (usually on the filter) and hook up your air hose to the out-take (often the lubricator).

For permanent installations like the one shown in the drawing

above, I suggest running copper or galvanized pipe from the compressor to the filter/regulator assembly. This allows you to create separate lines for tools that require lubrication (like drills and impact wrenches) and spraying equipment, where the air must be oil-free to prevent contaminating the finish.

It's also a good idea to install a shutoff valve such as a gate valve between the compressor and the filter/regulator assembly, in case you want to be able to disconnect the air hose without first emptying the tank of the compressor.

Two additional things here. First, regardless whether you use copper or galvanized pipe, make sure to slope the piping toward the compressor to help condensation moisture drain safely away (*see*

page 47). Second, install petcocks or valves at the low points of the system, and drain them whenever you drain the moisture out of your compressor (for more on this, *see page 86*).

REGULATORS

A regulator is installed between a compressor and an air tool so that you can control the pressure going to the tool. Most models have a built-in gauge so you can monitor the outgoing pressure and provide a regulated output from 0 to 150 psi (pounds per square inch).

Regulators are rated according to the maximum pressure (psi) and maximum airflow or cfm they can safely handle. It's important to note that regulators can't increase the psi above the incoming pressure.

Some compressors have a built-in regulator, but these are often both cheaply made and inaccessible. For permanent installations, it's well worth the cost to install a separate high-quality regulator. It'll last longer and be easier to adjust, and you can mount it in a convenient location.

In a typical setup, air from the compressor first passes though an air filter (*see opposite page*), then through the regulator (this removes any impurities before the air passes through the more-delicate regulator parts, like the diaphragm).

The intake and outtake ports on the regulator should be clearly labeled. Make sure to wrap several turns of Teflon tape around the nipple threads that connect the separate parts before assembling.

Adjusting the knob on a regulator (*see drawing at right*) varies the tension on an internal spring that presses against a rubber diaphragm. The pressure from the diaphragm, combined with the incoming air, forces the regulator body up and down, and along with it the regulator valve, thereby controlling the outgoing air pressure.

Most regulators have an additional nut on the adjusting rod so that you can lock the pressure in at a given setting—a nice feature to look for when buying a regulator.

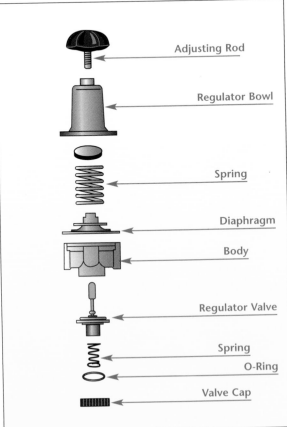

Adjusting Rod

Regulator Bowl

Spring

Diaphragm

Body

Regulator Valve

Spring

O-Ring

Valve Cap

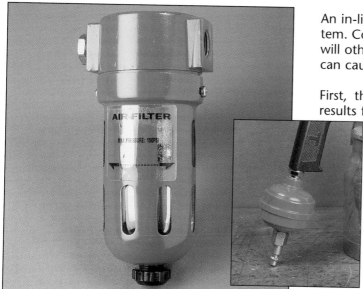

An in-line filter is a must on any compressed air system. Contaminants in the form of oil, water, and dirt will otherwise flow unchecked to your air tools. This can cause a horde of problems.

First, the inevitable water from condensation that results from compressing air will harm any tool you use. To prevent your tools from rusting from the inside out, it's imperative to remove this water.

Dirt from a compressor or the air lines is also bad for your tools. Small bits of metal or rust can clog up an intake port, thereby reducing pressure and efficiency. At the same time, it can cake internal parts—creating friction, excessive wear, and eventually tool failure.

Although there's a special accessory—a lubricator—that can inject oil periodically into the air line (*see page 22*), not all tools require oil (self-lubricating nail guns, for example). In the case of spraying on finishes, oil in the line will contaminate the finish, and you can end up with a ruined project. A quality in-line filter will remove oil along with water and dirt.

Although designed to supplement an in-line filter and not replace one, a disposable spray gun filter (*inset*) can be used in a pinch to remove oil and water from an air line. This type of filter simply screws onto the air inlet of the spray gun, and the air line is hooked up to it.

There are two main types of in-line filters available: separators and mechanical filters. The most common is separator (*see drawing at left*), which uses a whirlpool effect to trap contaminants as they flow through a chamber. A drain valve on the bottom of the chamber allows you to clean out contaminants.

Mechanical filters pass air through an absorbing material, usually in the form of a cartridge. This type of filter must be periodically replaced when it becomes clogged.

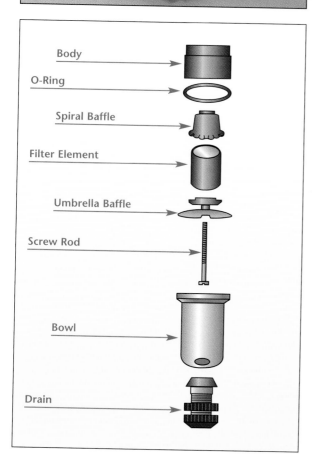

Body

O-Ring

Spiral Baffle

Filter Element

Umbrella Baffle

Screw Rod

Bowl

Drain

Air Tools

IN-LINE LUBRICATOR

An in-line lubricator (or oiler) can be placed between the compressor and the air line to inject tiny droplets of oil in the line periodically. This is a good thing: Most air tools require periodic lubrication, and a self-dispensing oil lubricator will make your air tools virtually maintenance-free. If a filter and regulator are being used, the lubricator is installed after them.

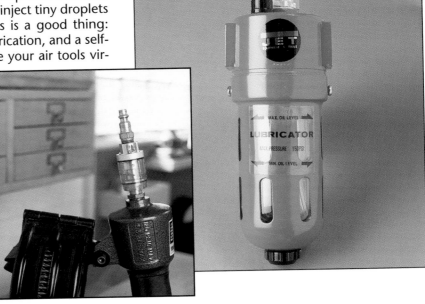

Warning: If you're planning on using your compressor to power a spray gun, do not install a lubricator on the main line. If you want to use both a lubricator and spraying equipment, install a separate line (*see page 19*) and use a hose that's dedicated to spraying.

If you don't, oil in the line will mix with and contaminate the finish, possibly ruining your project (and your day). Another option is to use a small in-line oiler (*see inset*) that is attached to the end of the air line and hooks directly to the tool you want lubricated.

Most lubricators have clear bowls so you can quickly check the oil level and a set of marks to indicate when you need to add oil (pneumatic tool oil is available wherever air tools are sold—do not use motor oil in its place).

Adjusting the knob on the lubricator (*see drawing at right*) lets you control how many drops of oil per minute are added to the air. The drops of oil, when mixed with air, create a mist that flows out through the air line to lubricate your tools.

As the oil moves through the tools, it leaves a film that creates a seal between parts. It also helps to push or move dirt out of the lines, tools, and motor. The oil can even act as a coolant in some tools to help dissipate heat.

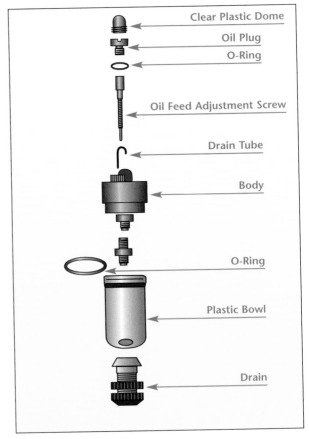

Clear Plastic Dome

Oil Plug

O-Ring

Oil Feed Adjustment Screw

Drain Tube

Body

O-Ring

Plastic Bowl

Drain

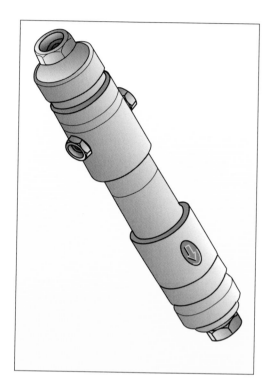

Whenever air is compressed, water vapor in the air condenses. In some instances, such as spraying finishes, water in the line can cause defects and surface blemishes. A filter will remove some of the water vapor; and although a dryer won't eliminate all of it, it will reduce it enough so it won't affect your finishes.

For most homeowners, an in-line filter is sufficient. However, if you live in a humid region or if you're planning on spraying a lot of finish, you may want to consider a dryer.

All dryers work on the same principle: They remove moisture from the air by developing a dewpoint temperature (the temperature where water vapor in the air turns liquid) that's lower than the lowest temperature in the air line dowstream.

There are four basic types of dryers: refrigerated, deliquescent, regenerative desiccant, and membrane-type. Refrigerated dryers are large and expensive and are used in industrial applications. Deliquescent dryers force air to flow through a chemical that melts away as it absorbs water vapor. Regenerative desiccant dryers use desiccant beads to attract water and trap it.

The three dryers described so far are very expensive. A lower-cost alternative is a membrane-type dryer like the one shown here. Air passes through a semipermeable hollow membrane fiber, while water vapor diffuses through fiber walls (*see drawing below*).

Suitable for a homeowner, most membrane dryers can handle air volumes up to 150 cfm, are lightweight enough to be installed in piping without additional support, and work with no moving parts and no power source.

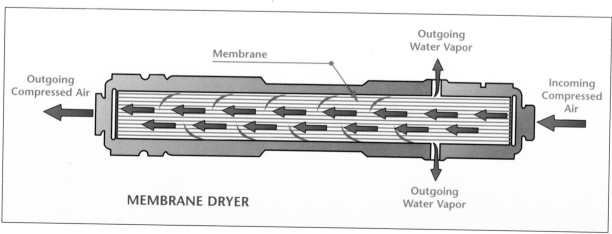

MEMBRANE DRYER

HOSES

Standard Most standard air hose is made of PVC and is rated to handle from 150 to 300 psi. Relatively inexpensive, PVC hose resists lubricating oils and sunlight, and it remains flexible over a wide range of temperatures. All standard air hoses come with threaded fittings, typically either ¼" or ⅜" NPT threads (*see page 25*). Lengths vary from 25 up to 100 feet, or you can purchase bulk rolls of up to 500 feet.

Higher-quality hoses are made of neoprene rubber and are reinforced with braided polyester. As you'd suspect, they're considerably more expensive, but they last longer.

Lightweight plastic Popular in the construction trades, clear plastic hose is rugged yet lightweight. The weight of a hose may not seem like a big deal, but after you've lugged a heavy hose around all day, you'll be dreaming of ways to pare down the weight.

A lightweight hose will help considerably, but not without exacting a price. This type of hose isn't as flexible as standard hose and has the annoying habit of not lying flat—it often gets tangled around your feet. That's unsafe on the ground, and just plain hazardous on scaffolding.

Recoil Retractable recoil hose in its familiar yellow color is standard in shops and plants around the world. Quite often it's attached to an air line running along the ceiling. Grab it and pull it down when you need it. It recoils up out of the way when you're done.

Recoil hose is commonly available in 25- and 50-foot lengths. Most have swivel-type fittings on the end, with attached spring guards to help prevent kinks in the hose. Here again, they come with either ¼" or ⅜" NPT threads.

Threaded The most common type of fitting used for air hose and tools is the brass threaded fitting. This is a screw-type fitting that's tightened with a wrench. Typical sizes are ¼" and ⅜" NPT threads.

Whenever you connect a threaded fitting to a tool, hose, or other fitting (such as a quick-connect; *see below*), make sure to wrap a couple turns of Teflon tape around the threads to ensure a leakproof seal.

Quick-connect Quick-connect fittings let you connect and disconnect tools from the air line without having to shut down the compressor. That's because the female half of the male-female coupling pair has a built-in shutoff valve. This makes the female coupling considerably more expensive than the male.

Although quick-connect fittings are typically sold in pairs of male and female couplings, they're also available individually. A word to the wise here: Pick one brand of coupling and stick with it—not all quick-connect fittings can be interchanged.

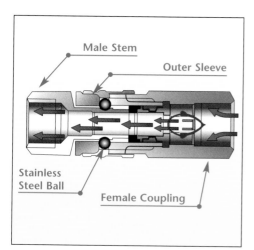

Male Stem

Outer Sleeve

Stainless
Steel Ball

Female Coupling

Cross section of a quick-connect A male coupling (*left*) threads onto a tool, and a female (*right*) threads onto the air source. When the couplings are joined together, the air will flow freely. When they're disconnected, a shutoff inside the female coupling automatically turns off the air flow.

To use a quick-connect fitting, pull back the outer sleeve on the female coupling and insert the male coupling stem. Push the stem in and release the outer sleeve. You'll notice a quick burst of air as the seal is temporarily opened and then closed.

SPRAY GUNS

If you've ever spent all weekend painting a fence or a couple weekends painting a house by hand, it should come as no surprise to find that spray guns are one of the most popular accessories for a compressor. But spray guns are capable of atomizing a lot more than paint: You can spray stains and dyes, clear finishes (like varnish, shellac, and lacquer), even adhesives like contact cement (this is how most cabinet manufacturers apply adhesive).

Spray guns come in many types and styles. Two of the most common types are shown here: a standard siphon-feed gun for general-purpose spraying (*left in photo*) and a detail sprayer for fine work and touch-up jobs (*right in photo*).

Spray guns are classified in a number of ways. First, whether the material to be sprayed is mixed inside the air cap (internal mix) or outside the air cap (external mix); *see page 27.* Second, how the material you're spraying is fed through the tip: siphon, pressure, or gravity (*see page 28*). And finally, whether the air flowing to the tip is continuous or is controlled by the trigger (bleeder or nonbleeder, respectively).

The first step in selecting a spray gun is to determine what type of materials you'll likely be spraying. Lightweight materials like stain can be sprayed successfully with a relatively inexpensive gun. Heavier materials like varnish and paint require a higher-quality, more expensive spray gun.

A high-quality gun (costing $100 to $300) will offer a wide variety of fluid tips and air caps (*see drawing below*) that can be used in different combinations to spray almost anything. Spraying heavier materials also requires a heavy-duty air compressor—one capable of producing up to 15 to 20 cfm.

Check with the manufacturer of the spray gun to see if the gun you have in mind is capable of spraying the materials you want. Most reputable manufacturers have charts available that list the correct fluid tip/air cap combination for specific materials.

ANATOMY OF A SPRAY GUN

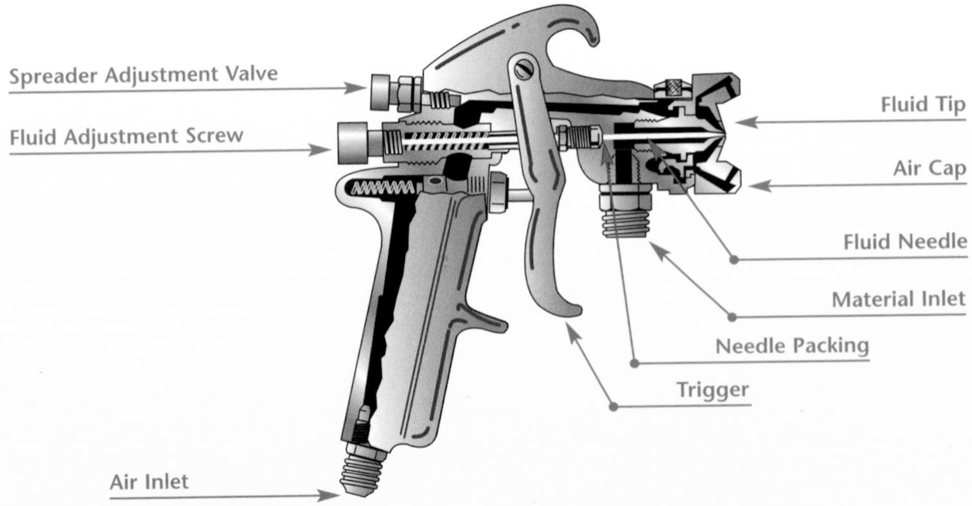

Spreader Adjustment Valve

Fluid Adjustment Screw

Fluid Tip

Air Cap

Fluid Needle

Material Inlet

Needle Packing

Trigger

Air Inlet

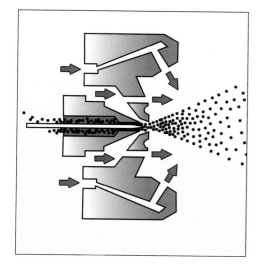

External mix In an external-mix air cap, the spray gun mixes and atomizes the material to be sprayed outside the air cap. An external-mix cap is easily identified by the pair of tips that project out of the cap face (*see drawing at left*).

Air is pushed out of small ports in the two tips and from around the fluid tube to atomize the material delivered by the tube. This type of air cap is particularly useful for fast-drying finishes that would quickly gum up and clog an internal-mix cap (*see below*).

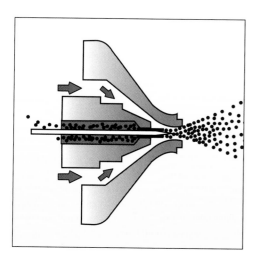

Internal mix An internal-mix air cap doesn't have projecting tips, since the material is mixed with air to atomize it inside the cap right before it is ejected. As you can see in the drawing, the fluid tip in an internal-mix cap sits well back of the opening in the cap.

Internal-mix caps work well for slow-drying materials (never use an internal mix cap with a fast-drying finish), or where low pressure is available (such as applying paint to the exterior of a house with a small compressor), or when a low volume of material is needed.

CAP PATTERNS

A round-pattern cap (*left*) is the most common pattern, as it's found on most external-mix air caps. This style of cap is often referred to as a "low bounce" cap, as the majority of the material being sprayed hits and stays on target. This makes it particularly suitable for odd-shaped parts such as lawn furniture. A fan pattern (*right*), common on many internal-mix caps, sprays a fan-shaped pattern that's useful for covering large, flat surfaces, such as interior walls, exterior walls, and tabletops.

Air Tools

FEED TYPES

Siphon feed A siphon (or suction) feed spray gun is easily identifiable by the material cup located below the gun. A siphon gun uses compressed air to create a vacuum at the air cap. Atmospheric pressure acting on the material in the cup forces the material up the siphon tube. From there it travels into the gun and out through the fluid tip, where it's atomized by the air cap.

Siphon guns typically come with a 1-quart cup—more than enough for small jobs like staining a piece of furniture or applying a coat of paint to a bicycle.

Pressure feed When you need to spray a lot of material, the material is heavy, or you need to apply material fast, a pressure-feed gun is the way to go.

With this type of system, the fluid tip is flush with the air cap, and the material to be sprayed is pressurized in a separate container located away from the gun—usually a tank that resembles a pressure cooker (*see page 29*). The air pressure forces the material through the material line into the gun and out the air cap, where it is atomized.

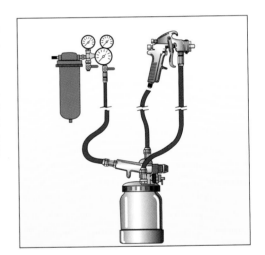

Gravity feed Gravity-feed guns are also easy to identify, because the material holder is mounted on top. Because of problems with weight and balance, the material holders are limited to a half-pint or 1-pint capacity.

Since there's no need for a fluid pickup tube, a gravity-feed gun is very reliable—as long as the vent hole in the top of the holder is kept open. Also, as no pressure is needed to force material into the gun, gravity-feed sprayers require less incoming air—which means they can be used with smaller compressors.

Cups Material cups typically come in 1-quart capacities for siphon feed guns (*right in photo*) and half-pint and 1-pint capacities for gravity-feed guns and detail sprayers (*left in photo*). These cups are used where relatively small quantities of material are being sprayed.

Most cups attach to the gun with either clamps or screws. You'll also find pressure-feed cups—commonly in 1- and 2-quart sizes. If you're planning on spraying a variety of materials, I'd suggest buying extra cups: one for clear finishes and one for colored materials.

Tanks Pressure tanks are great for those larger jobs where you need to spray a lot of material. It's amazing how much time you can save by not constantly having to refill a small material cup.

A typical pressure tank consists of a shell or body; a clamp-on lid that resembles a pressure cooker; a fluid tube and header; and a regulator, gauge, and pressure-relief valve. They're available with either top or bottom fluid outlets and with various accessories, like an agitator to keep heavy-pigment material in motion and liners to make cleanup easy.

Fluid hose A fluid or material hose is designed specifically to carry material from a pressurized tank or cup to a spray gun.

Safety Note: Do not use standard air hose to transfer materials, in particular solvent-based fluids. The solvents in these materials will attack and destroy regular rubber compounds in standard hose.

Fluid hose is constructed with special nylon solvent-resistant materials that are impervious to the most common solvents. Many manufacturers suggest limiting the length of this type of hose to 50 feet.

Air Tools

AIRBRUSHES

When most folks think about an airbrush, the image that often comes to mind is of an artist custom-spraying T-shirts at a county or state fair, or an auto detailer adding the final touches to classic car. But airbrushes can be used for all sorts of projects. They're terrific for detail work that a spray gun or even a detail sprayer is incapable of.

Airbrushes provide pinpoint control of the fluid stream and allow you add a wide variety of effects to your projects. If you're a woodworker and have ever considered trying to add "tone" to a finish, an airbrush is the perfect tool. Likewise, toymakers, model makers, and furniture restorers will find this an invaluable tool.

There are two main types of airbrush, the single-action and the dual-action; *see below.* Both run on a pressure between 15 and 50 psi, with 30 psi generally accepted as the optimum pressure. Because of this low pressure requirement, many airbrush users find that a small, tankless compressor is more than sufficient.

Single-action The trigger on a single-action airbrush controls the airflow like a light switch—the air is either on or off. When the trigger is depressed, a preset amount of fluid is sprayed. You can adjust the amount of fluid being sprayed via the needle adjustment screw, located on the back of the handle.

The pattern that both a single-action and a dual-action airbrush will produce can be adjusted by rotating the fluid cap at the front of the airbrush: typically, clockwise for less fluid, counter-clockwise for more.

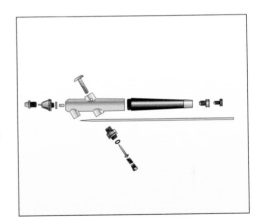

Dual-action Unlike its simpler cousin, the trigger on a dual-action airbrush controls both the airflow and the fluid supply—down for air, back for more fluid. This allows you to vary the width of line or change the opacity of the paint with a single motion.

With the single-action brush, you'd have to stop your motion to regulate the fluid. No wonder this is the tool of choice for professionals. Just like spray guns, airbrushes are available with internal- or external-mix caps and can use either gravity feed or siphon feed.

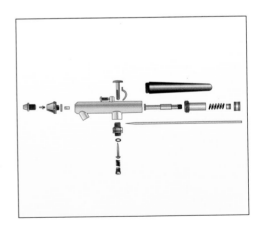

Sandblaster One of the quickest ways to remove paint, rust, and stubborn dirt from exterior walls or outdoor furniture is to blast it off with sand. A typical sandblaster kit for a compressor comes with a sandblast gun, a 10-foot flexible rubber feed hose, and a pickup tube.

One thing to look for when buying a sandblaster is to make sure that replacement nozzles are readily available. High-velocity sand moving through even a quality nozzle will quickly wear; the opening will enlarge and efficiency will be lost (*see pages 49–50* for more on sandblasting).

Sand hopper When portability is required, a sand hopper with a shoulder strap is just the ticket. The hopper shown here will hold 30 pounds of sand. It's the perfect size for carrying up a ladder or working from scaffolding to tackle jobs like sandblasting soffits, or removing paint from the second-story exterior walls of a house. The only requirement is for a long air hose.

Larger hoppers with wheels are available; these can hold anywhere from 60 to 120 pounds of sand. Hoppers typically require 7 to 10 cfm at 90 psi.

Pressure washer A pressure washer will make quick work of removing dirt and grime from a variety of surfaces. It combines the power of compressed air with water and detergent to spray clean things like campers, cars, gutters, lawn furniture, sidewalks, and windows.

Most pressure-washer kits for compressors consist of a gun and a chemical draw hose that's inserted in a container of detergent. To work properly, a typical pressure washer requires a compressor that's at least 1 hp (or larger) and that's capable of producing around 5 cfm at 90 psi.

Air Tools

PORTABLE AIR TOOLS

Sanders Since I started using air-powered sanders, their electric cousins just collect dust on a shelf. That's because air sanders are quieter (no irritating high-pitched whine), run cooler, are smaller and lighter, yet have plenty of power.

Shown here *clockwise from top right:* a jitterbug sander, a random-orbit sander, and a straight-line sander (*see pages 53–54* for more on sanders). The only disadvantage is that air sanders need a lot of air to work properly, typically 6 to 10 cfm at 90 psi—which calls for at least a 3-hp compressor.

Die grinders Although die grinders have been used in industry for years, they're rapidly being used more and more in home workshops. Their aggressive abrasive action will quickly remove even the most stubborn rust. They're also handy for sharpening cutting tools.

Most die grinders come with a selection of abrasive wheels and "points" that slip into either a ⅛" or ¼" collet. Smaller die grinders require 3 to 6 cfm at 90 psi, while the heavy-duty or "industrial" versions need upwards of 12 cfm.

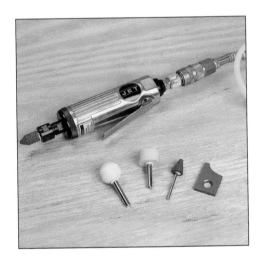

Drills Since air-powered tools don't require a separate motor, they're smaller than their electric counterparts. That's one of the biggest advantages to an air drill: A smaller size lets you get into corners and hard-to-reach places that an electric drill just can't handle.

Their compact size also makes it easy to "get behind" the drill and efficiently transfer your body weight to the drill for those heavy-duty boring jobs. A typical air drill requires around 3 to 4 cfm at 90 psi. They're also available with variable speed and keyless chucks.

Impact wrenches An impact wrench is an air-powered, reversible, hand-held wrench. When the trigger is depressed, the output shaft and socket attached to it spin freely between 2,500 and 15,000 rpm. When the socket meets resistance, a small spring-loaded hammer strikes an anvil attached to the drive shaft. This moves the socket until the nut is free.

Safety Note: Make sure to use only impact-rated sockets with an impact wrench: Standard sockets can't withstand the percussion that these heavy-duty sockets can, and they'll break and fly apart.

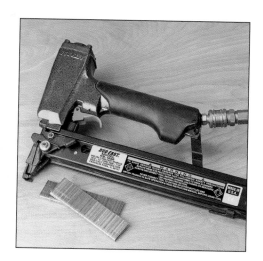

Staplers Air-powered staplers are a great addition to any workshop. They're terrific for jobs where you need extra holding power but where the staple won't show, such as for upholstery or attaching the back to a cabinet.

Medium- and light-duty staplers typically hold many more fasteners than a finish nailer (*see page 36*). Staples are 18 gauge and ¼", ⅜", or ⁷⁄₁₆" in width, with lengths varying from ⅜" to 1½". Heavy-duty staplers (usually 15 or 16 gauge) can handle even tough jobs like attaching roof shingles and wall sheathing.

Screwdrivers Just like an air-powered drill, a pneumatic screwdriver is smaller than its electric counterpart but just as powerful. Here again, this makes it ideal for cramped spaces.

As with an electric driver, most air screwdrivers come with an adjustable clutch that allows you to drive a screw flush with a surface without stripping or breaking the screw. Many screwdrivers also have quick-change chucks that accept standard ¼" hex bits. Typical air consumption for an air screwdriver is 3 to 4 cfm at 90 psi.

FRAMING NAILERS

I know I shouldn't admit this, but I can't hammer a nail for beans. It's a good thing I'm a woodworker and not a carpenter—I rarely use metal fasteners at all, and when I do, it's a screw. But I do use nails for construction, and I've found that I'm using finish nails and brads more now, with the added precision that most air guns offer.

When I first saw a framing nailer in use, I knew I had to have one. I was visiting a finish carpenter friend at a construction site and I noticed a fellow toenailing studs in a wall. If you've ever tried this, you know how difficult it is to hold a stud in perfect position as you nail it in place: Every time you hit the nail, the stud moves—very frustrating.

When I saw the carpenter toenail with a framing nailer, the stud didn't move at all—and the nail was set in just the perfect amount. That's because a framing nailer literally shoots the nail into the wood in one quick motion.

Framing nailers are indispensable for those jobs where you've got a lot of nails to drive, such as putting up walls, laying new floors or sheathing, or for roofing.

Any nail gun that shoots 6d to 16d (2"- to 3½"-long) nails is classified as a framing nailer. Framing nailers are further defined by the type of magazine they use to hold fasteners; *see the sidebar below.*

MAGAZINE TYPES: STRAIGHT VS. COIL

There are two basic ways fasteners are fed into a framing nailer: The most common, *at left,* **is a straight magazine (or stick);** *at right* **is a coil magazine. Each has its advantages and disadvantages. A gun with a stick magazine is much lighter and far more maneuverable than one with a coil magazine. But a coil magazine offers greater fastener storage (typically 150 to 300 coils versus 50-nail strips), which means fewer reloads.**

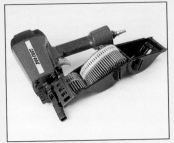

ANATOMY OF AN AIR NAILER

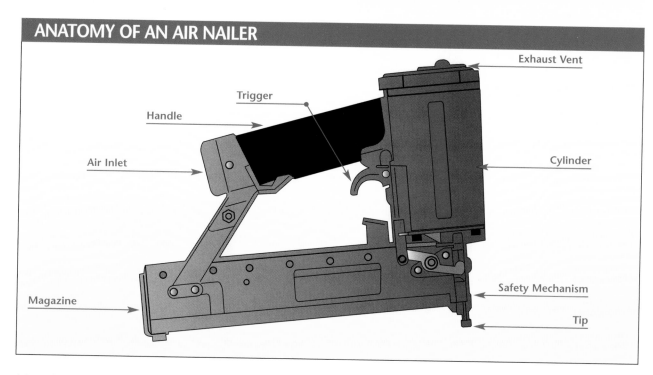

Exhaust Vent
Trigger
Handle
Air Inlet
Cylinder
Magazine
Safety Mechanism
Tip

Most framing nailers work on the same principle: When the trigger is depressed and the nosepiece is engaged by pressing the gun against a workpiece, a blast of air is injected into the cylinder in the head. This forces the piston with the driving blade attached to it down to strike the nail and drive it into the workpiece; *see the drawing above.*

Framing nailers are not cheap: A quality one will cost between $400 and $600. So it's important to buy a brand you trust. Duo-fast, Senco, Hitachi, Porter-Cable, Paslode, and Bostitch all make quality guns. If you can justify the cost (or like me, you've just got to have one), another decision you'll have to make is what type of fastener you want to shoot.

Most nailers shoot either a roundhead or clipped-head nail. Clipped (or D-head) nails have part of the head trimmed off so more can be packed in a magazine. I prefer full roundhead nails, as they offer better shear strength. Also, clipped-head nails are not approved in all locales, so make sure you check your local building code before buying a clipped-head nailer.

Finally, the type of contact point or tip that comes with a an air nailer will determine how much of a dent, if any, the nailer leaves after shooting a nail (*see the sidebar at left*).

CONTACTS FOR AIR NAILERS

Loop: A rounded loop contact works best for attaching shaped or profiled moldings. The rounded edges of the loop slip easily into details, allowing the nail to be driven well below the surface.

Cushion: A cushioned contact is best suited for flat work that you don't want to mar, as when installing baseboards. Note: You can remove the cushion to get in tight to a corner.

Sheet metal: The bent sheet metal contact, although commonly described as a no-mar tip, will often dent and gouge most woods. I would steer clear of these whenever possible.

FINISH NAILERS

If you're not interested in framing and construction but you often do trim or finish work, a finish nailer will make the job a whole lot easier. Not as beefy as a framing nailer, a finish nailer shoots 15- and 16-gauge nails varying in length from ¾" to 2¾".

This makes them ideal for attaching trim, chair railing (*as shown*), crown molding, window and door casings, and so forth. A professional model can easily cost $400, while a less expensive, imported version can be purchased for less that half that.

When looking to buy a finish nailer, the first choice you need to make is what gauge nail to shoot. Thinner, 16-gauge nails are less likely to split wood than the heavier 15-gauge. But the disadvantage to the smaller gauge is that the nails tend to follow the grain in wood and often deflect off course, sometimes protruding out the face.

Additional features to look for are whether the magazine is straight or angled (*see the sidebar below*) and how the fasteners load into the magazine (*see the sidebar on page 37*). While a typical framing nailer requires 4 to 6 cfm at 90 psi, a finish nailer can get by with around half that.

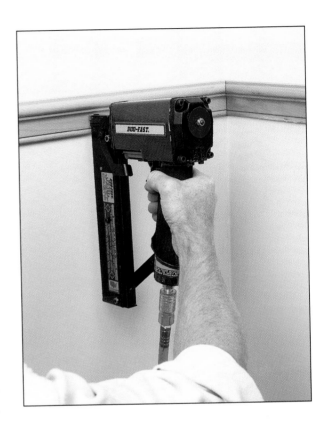

ANGLED AND STRAIGHT MAGAZINES

As a general rule of thumb, 15-gauge nailers (*left*) have angled magazines, while 16-gauge nailers (*right*) come with straight magazines. You can, however, find both 15- and 16-gauge nailers with either a straight or an angled magazine. I prefer an angled magazine because it lets me get into corners and other tight spots that a straight magazine can't navigate, such as applying crown molding around the ceiling perimeter of a room.

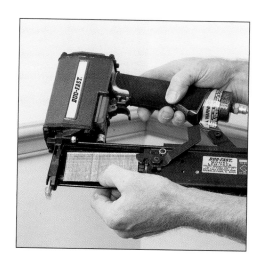

Rear-load Most angled-magazine nailers (like the one shown) load their fasteners in from the rear. To load nails into this type of gun, first disconnect the air from the tool and then release the latch at the rear of the magazine. Then pull back on the magazine's spring.

Now you can load in a strip of nails and snap the cover back in place. The magazine's spring will now advance the nail strip into the firing position.

Side-load The majority of a straight-magazine nailers load their fasteners in from the side. I've always found this type of nailer very easy to load.

Here again, with the air disconnected, release the magazine latch. This time, though, the latch can be at either the front or the rear of the magazine. When the latch is released, slide back the magazine and insert a strip of nails. Then just slide back the magazine until the latch engages. What could be simpler?

NO-MAR TIPS

Virtually all finish nailers come with a "no-mar" tip. There is quite a difference, however, in the different types of tips and their ability to prevent dings and dents. The two most common no-mar tips are the rubber tip (*left*) and the bent sheet metal tip (*right*). In my experience, the rubber cushioned tip does a much better job of protecting wood surfaces than the sheet metal tip.

NARROW CROWN STAPLERS

Basic use Narrow crown staplers, like the one shown, are gaining rapidly in popularity among homeowners, especially those who enjoy working with wood. The most common staplers shoot ¼" or ⅜" staples in gauges ranging from 16 to 22.

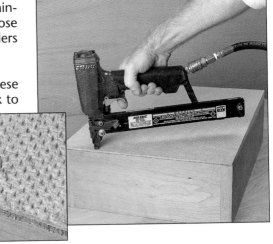

Light-duty staplers require only 1 to 2 cfm at 90 psi, so these can be used with smaller compressors. The major drawback to using a staple is its footprint (*inset*). As it's difficult to hide the head of staple, they're primarily used in areas that won't be seen.

Staple types There are a wide variety of staples to choose from. Shown here *from top to bottom* are: a chisel staple that's good for dense materials; a divergent outside bevel staple that couples excellent holding power with a locking action; a divergent staple, where the legs diverge for a better hold in soft woods; an inside bevel staple, which clinches the staple outward in medium-dense materials; an outside bevel staple that clinches inward; and a blunt staple for very dense materials where you're concerned about cracking or fracturing.

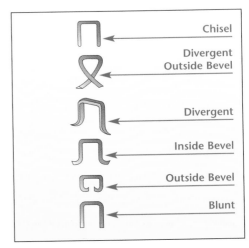

Chisel

Divergent Outside Bevel

Divergent

Inside Bevel

Outside Bevel

Blunt

HOLDING POWER OF STAPLES

One reason that staples afford such great holding power is that the legs of the staple often splay out when the staple is shot into the wood. This offers a much better mechanical advantage over a conventional nail.

Not all staples will splay (*see above*), and the density of the material you're shooting into will have an impact on whether the legs will splay at all and, if they do, how much.

Versatile Of all the air guns out there, I use my brad nailer more often than all the others combined. That's because a brad nailer is so versatile: It can tack on molding strips, affix drawer bottoms, quickly assemble jigs and fixtures—just about anything.

Brad nailers typically shoot 18-gauge brads that can vary in length from ⅝" to 1½". Unlike many nailers that only shoot one size of nail, most brad nailers can shoot brads of varying length. Just pick the right length for the job, and load it into the magazine.

Ease of loading Most brad nailers are simple to load. Many feature a side loading system where all you do (once the air line is disconnected from the tool) is pull down a hinged magazine cover, or slide it to one side, and drop in a strip of brads. Snap the cover back in place, hook up the air, and you're ready to go.

Quick Tip: Keep your fasteners as clean as possible. Any debris (such as sawdust or dirt) can build up inside the head of the gun and eventually lead to a jam.

FASTENER SELECTION CHART

Fastener Type	Application	Size
Staples	upholstery	22 gauge, ³⁄₁₆" – ⁹⁄₁₆"
	case construction	19 gauge, ¼" – 1"
	roof sheathing	16 gauge 1" – 2"
	subflooring	15 gauge, 1½" – 2½"
Roundhead nails	framing	12d–16d, 2" – 3¼"
	decking	12d–16d, 2" – 3¼"
	wall sheathing	12d–16d, 2¼" – 3"
	fencing	8d–12d, 1¾" – 2¾"
Finish nails	furniture work	16 gauge, 1" – 2"
	cabinet assembly	15 gauge, 1¼" – 2½"
	trim	15 gauge, 1¼" – 2½"
Brads	paneling	20 gauge, ⅝" – 1"
	light trim	20 gauge, 1" – 1⁹⁄₁₆"
	light assembly	20 gauge, 1" – 1⁹⁄₁₆"

Air Tools

SAFETY FEATURES OF NAILERS

Air nailers are powerful tools that can greatly speed up your work and can possibly add a higher level of precision to it. But power like this comes with a price.

There's no doubt about it—air nailers are dangerous tools. Any just like any other powerful tool, you need to develop both a healthy respect for the tool and a series of safety habits that will become second nature to you (*see pages 68–69* for more on this).

Air-nailer manufacturers have built a number of safety features into their nailers. But to me the big difference is whether the nailer is sequential or contact-trip activated; *see below and page 41.*

Another safety feature, although not all that common, is a nailer that uses dual triggers; *see page 41.*

Sequential-trip A sequential-trip nailer requires you to press the nosepiece of the nailer firmly against the workpiece with your finger off the trigger. This depresses the sequential-trip safety mechanism, which allows you to pull the trigger and drive a nail.

Depending on the manufacturer, this means that you have to release the trigger after each nail is driven and/or lift up the nailer so that the sequential-trip mechanism clears. This action is repeated for every nail fired; compare this with the contact (touch) trip shown on page 41.

WHAT'S MORE IMPORTANT TO YOU: SPEED OR SAFETY?

The big question when deciding on safety features of an air nailer is what's more important to you: speed or safety? A sequential-trip air nailer gets the best marks for built-in safety, but it'll definitely slow you down. A contact or trip mechanism allows you to bounce-fire, which is a lot faster than a sequential trip. For me, there's no debate—I choose safety. I'm just never in that much of a hurry.

I have a carpenter friend who accidentally shot a nail in the leg of a coworker with a trip-contact nailer. He and his buddy were laying shingles on a roof. His buddy was positioning the shingles, and he was bounce-nailing like crazy. Near the edge of the roof, he slipped and touched the nosepiece of the nailer to his buddy's leg. Because he had the trigger depressed, it discharged a nail. This wouldn't have happened with a sequential-trip mechanism.

Contact- or touch-trip Unlike a sequential-trip mechanism, a contact- or touch-trip mechanism allows you to leave the trigger depressed between nails. This way all you have to do is engage the safety mechanism by pushing it down against the workpiece.

This method is often referred to as "bounce" firing because it allows you to keep the tool moving along the work surface with a bouncing motion, depressing the safety mechanism wherever you want to drive a nail or staple.

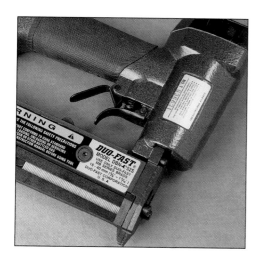

Two triggers Another safety feature is a nailer with two triggers. A dual-trigger nailer takes some getting used to, as you must depress both triggers to drive a nail or brad.

To use this type of nailer, place it where you want to drive a nail, and depress one trigger, then the other. The nailer will fire when the triggers are depressed in any sequence.

Note that this type of nailer doesn't need to be pushed down to release a safety. For this reason, these nailers offer excellent no-mar characteristics.

SAFETY GLASSES

There are two good reasons that virtually every air nailer you can buy comes with a pair of safety glasses. First, all nailers need to exhaust spent air after a nail has been driven. On most nailers (like the one *shown here*), this exhaust vent is at the top of the gun. And since you're usually looking where the nails are going, the gun is often right in front of your face. A blast of air directed toward your eyes, especially in a dusty or dirty environment, can be dangerous. Second, when a nail is shot into a workpiece, fragments can and do break off and go flying in all directions. It's absolutely imperative that you develop a habit of donning safety glasses or goggles before you even pick up an air nailer.

COST RANGES

I've concentrated on two major air tools here, spray guns and air nailers, because there's such a wide selection of each type and a correspondingly varied range of cost. The charts shown here list a general price range for each tool and are intended only to give you an idea of approximate cost.

As with almost any tool purchase, you pretty much get what you pay for. The best advice I can give you is twofold. First, buy from a name you can trust. Look for a manufacturer that's been around for a while, and make sure that you can buy replacement parts. If you have access to the Internet, check out the company on-line to see whether they offer technical tips, service advice, and parts information.

Second, in my mind the old adage "cry once" certainly applies to tool buying. Dig deep and buy the best you can afford the first time: Try to get more than the minimum tool you need. This way it's likely you won't have to buy a more powerful or more flexible system later on.

Whenever possible, try to upgrade from a "hobbyist" grade to "professional." Although in many cases the tools will appear identical, the professional-grade tools offer higher-quality castings and materials. There's more attention to machining the parts and the overall fit and finish. The end result is a more reliable tool that, if well maintained, can last a lifetime.

AIR NAILERS

Type	Price Range
Framing	$350 – $800
Finish	$175 – $500
Stapler	$90 – $220
Brad	$90 – $150

SPRAY GUNS

Type	Price Range
Hobbyist	$35 – $65
Professional	$125 – $175
Detail	$40 – $75
Airbrush	$40 – $100

RECOMMENDATIONS

When it comes to my recommending an air nailer, four manufacturers come to mind, as they've all been around for a long time and all enjoy a well-deserved reputation for building quality tools: Duo-fast, Paslode, Senco, and Stanley-Bostitch. Choosing an air nailer really starts with defining the type of work you plan on doing. If a lot a framing work is in your future, a framing nailer (most likely with a straight magazine) is easy to justify. If, however, you'll need one only occasionally, you can rent one for around $35 a day from most rental stores. With the cost of a quality framing nailer well over $500, this may be the way to go.

Finishing nailer, stapler, or brad nailer? If your budget can afford it, I'd recommend a 16-guage finish nailer and an 18- to 20-gauge brad nailer, both with rubber no-mar tips. With these two tools, you can tackle almost any fastening job. If you're into upholstery, you'll definitely be better off with a narrow crown stapler.

It's easy for me to recommend a spray gun. I've used a Devilbiss for years, and it's still running smooth. This gun is virtually the standard in shops where quality work is being done. Devilbiss offers a huge variety of fluid needles and tips, which enables you to spray almost anything. If you don't need to spray a wide variety of materials, you can get by with a hobbyist grade, but I'd still recommend a professional sprayer. Most contractor paint stores stock common repair parts—something you'll appreciate when you're halfway through a job and your fluid tip wears out.

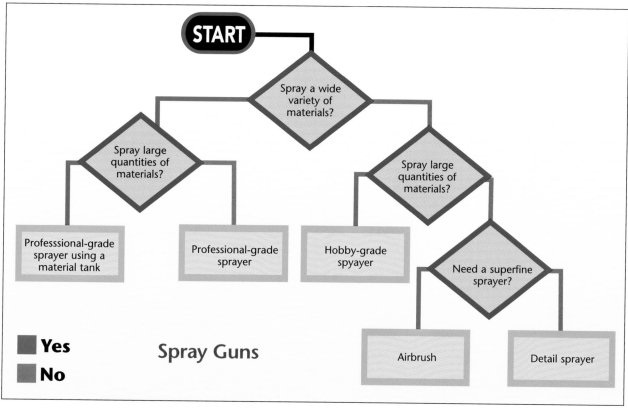

Spray Guns

■ Yes
■ No

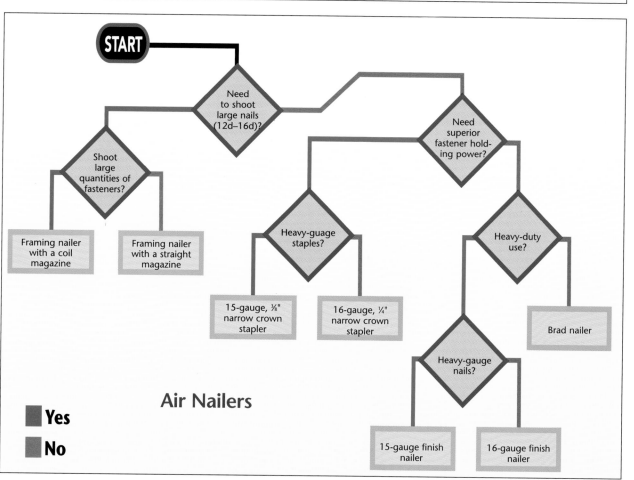

Air Nailers

■ Yes
■ No

CHAPTER 3

BASIC OPERATIONS

Bringing home a new compressor and a couple of air tools for the first time is similar to buying a new computer and some software. With a computer, there's a certain amount of hooking up and basic rules to learn before you can run the software that you bought the computer for in the first place. The same is true for a compressor and your air tools—you have to set it up and understand how it works before you can safely use the air tools.

But thankfully, setup and installation of a compressor is a whole lot simpler. And believe me, an air tool is a lot easier to operate than most of the software out there!

In this chapter, I'll start with setting up the compressor and system, beginning with defining the differences between a portable and a permanent setup. Then I'll take you through the steps necessary to set up a compressor in either a portable (*page 46*) or permanent (*pages 47–48*) installation. Everything from why you should use a longer air hose instead of an extension cord, to how much slope there should be in permanently installed air lines.

After that, I'll dive into the air tools that many homeowners are likely to first buy. To speed up the tedious chores of cleaning and scraping, there's a section on sandblasters (*pages 49–50*) and pressure washing (*pages 51–52*),

including selecting the proper grit to blast, what additive to use, and the optimum pressure.

Then on to some of my favorite air-powered tools—sanders. I'll describe the differences between the three most common types—random-orbit, jitterbug, and in-line—then cover the basic operation of each (*pages 53 and 54*).

Next, I'll go over how to use air-powered drills (*page 55*), impact wrenches (*page 56*), and die grinders (*page 57*).

The chapter concludes with a discussion of a simple but extremely useful air tool—the blow gun—and its many nozzles.

Your first task with a new compressor is setting up the system. If it's an oil-lubricated compressor, begin by adding quality compressor oil according to the manufacturer's instructions. Remove the dipstick and fill the crankcase with oil to the upper or full oil level mark—make sure the compressor is level for this. Note: Multi-viscosity oils are not recommended for air compressors. Oil-less compressors are ready to go right out of the box.

Before you plug in either variety, make sure that the pressure switch is off and that the air outlet of the compressor is connected to an air hose that's terminated either with a quick-connect fitting with an automatic shutoff or with an air tool.

Turn the pressure switch on and adjust the regulator to the desired pressure. Once the tank fills to the set pressure, the compressor should automatically turn off (unless it's a continuous-running tankless compressor). Further setup will depend on whether the compressor is intended for portable use or a permanent installation; *see below*.

Portable The advantage of a portable compressor setup is that your compressor will be ready to go at all times. Just carry or wheel it to the job site.

Instead of getting tangled in the air hose, I suggest you build or buy a hose caddy or reel that attaches to the compressor. The simple caddy shown not only keeps the hose out of harm's way, but also stores a favorite tool. (*See page 78* for detailed instuctions on how to make the caddy.) For more on portable compressor setup, *see page 46*.

Permanent Installing a compressor in a more permanent location doesn't mean it has to lose its portability (unless you bolt it to the floor to help dampen vibration; *see page 109*). With the judicious placement of a couple of quick-connect fittings, you can unhook the compressor and roll it away.

Simple installs like the one shown feature a wall-mounted regulator assembly and hose reel. More-permanent installations use copper pipe to extend air lines around the shop (for more on this, *see page 47*).

PORTABLE SETUP

Wheels If your portable compressor is the hand-carried variety (*left in drawing*), it's important that the pads on which the compressor rests are in good shape. Since they're typically made of soft rubber, it's easy for one to "pick up" a stray nail or screw. To prevent scratching floors, check the pads often to make sure that this hasn't happened. If any of the pads shows excessive wear, replace it immediately to ensure that the compressor stays level. On wheeled portable compressors (*right in drawing*), periodically check each wheel's mounting hardware and tighten if necessary.

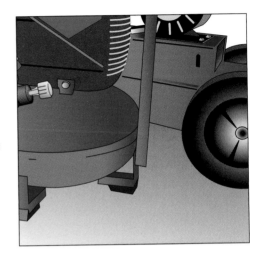

Hose Since you really can't use a compressor without a hose, I've always wondered why compressor manufacturers don't build in some kind of hose storage. This is especially true for transporting portable compressors, when your hands are often full with the compressor and assorted tools.

There are some aftermarket hose reels available, but they tend to be bulky and quite expensive. A simple solution is to build a shop-made caddy like the one shown. For construction details, *see page 78.*

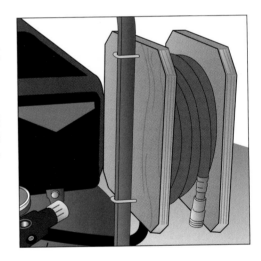

Don't use extension cords Whenever the electrical cord from your compressor doesn't reach an outlet—move it so it can reach, and use a longer air hose. Don't use an extension cord. Even small compressors draw substantial current from a circuit. The electrical cord on any quality compressor is beefy for a reason—to safely handle this heavy current.

Even if you've got an industrial-strength extension cord available, it will reduce the operating voltage and the compressor efficiency. You're better off with a longer air hose, as there is a negligible loss in hoses up to 100 feet.

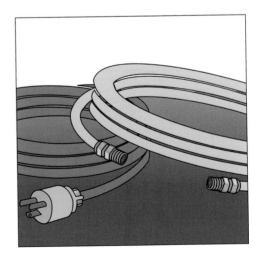

If you've got the space in your workshop, I heartily recommend setting your compressor up in a permanent location. This does a couple of things. First, you'll be more likely to use your air tools when a job comes up, because their power source will be right at hand. Second, it keeps everything organized and accessible so that the flip of a switch is all it takes make your air system ready to go. And third, by running pipe to various locations in your shop, you put air power at your fingertips—right where you need it.

For years, galvanized pipe was the choice for air lines. But the inevitable water in the pipes from condensation will cause the pipes to rust over time. Fittings start leaking and, even worse, rust chips break away and starting flowing along with the air to your tools. Not good. Two modern alternatives are copper and plastic pipe. I don't recommend plastic, because even if you use material rated to handle 120 psi, it will eventually leak. I prefer copper. I installed copper air lines in a shop over a decade ago, and they're still in perfect shape.

Location The most important decision you'll have to make concerning a permanent installation is where to put the compressor. In a perfect world, you'd have a separate room to muffle compressor noise; there'd be plenty of space to safely dissipate motor and pump heat and sufficient fresh air for it to breathe in and compress. Now, back to reality.

Try to locate the compressor where it can pull in copious amounts of fresh air and not build up heat. If your compressor is in a woodshop, consider adding a pre-filter over the compressor's air filter to help keep sawdust out.

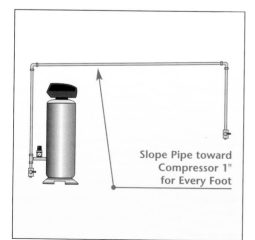

Slope Pipe toward
Compressor 1"
for Every Foot

Air line slope If you decide to run pipe in your shop, it's important that the lines slope back toward the compressor (roughly 1" of drop per every 12 feet in length). This way, condensation will drain harmlessly out of the system as long as you install a petcock on the drain, as shown (make sure to add a drain or petcock at the bottom of any vertical leg).

As a general rule of thumb, compressors up to 5 hp with lines less than 100 feet in length can get by with ¾" pipe, but check code for local sizing requirements.

Air Tools

Fittings One of the advantages to using copper air lines is that the fittings and joints are affixed with solder. Sweating copper pipe is fairly straightforward, and it provides both a strong and leak-proof joint.

As when running copper pipe for plumbing, make sure to ream the ends of the cut pipe to prevent restricted flow. Clean the pipe with emery cloth and the fittings with a brass brush. Make sure to use flux and a quality solder. If you prefer not to do this yourself, contact your local plumbing contractor.

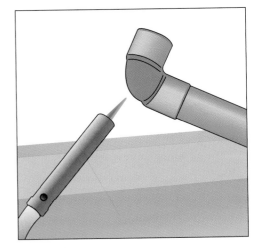

Separate regulator Even if your compressor has a built-in regulator, I'd suggest mounting a separate one up where you can get to it more easily. In most cases, you'll want to install a filter and possibly a lubricator anyway. Many "all-in-one" units are available, like the one shown here, that come already assembled: filter, regulator with gauge, and oiler.

Short "whip" hoses (typically 30" in length) with swivel fittings are a good choice for connecting the compressor to the regulator assembly.

Quick-connects For maximum flexibility of your air system, I recommend installing female quick-connect fittings on the ends of air hoses and the male counterparts on your air tools. This not only makes it easy to quickly connect and disconnect air tools, but also allows you to reconfigure your system quickly from job to job without reaching for an adjustable wrench to change a threaded fitting.

Pick one size and brand of quick-connect fitting and stick with it; not all connectors are interchangeable. (*See page 25* for more on these fittings.)

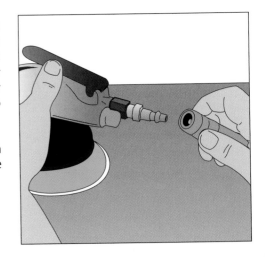

Setup Sandblasting cleans by abrading a surface with high-velocity particles. Although they're most often used to clean metal, sandblasters can also be used on wooden and masonry surfaces as long as care is taken.

Sand, aluminum oxide, and glass beads can all be used in a sandblaster; *see the chart on page 50* to match the material to the job. Since in most cases you'll be blasting for long periods of time, the larger the compressor and tank, the better.

Feed type There are two basic options for feeding sand into the blaster: a pickup tube (*shown here*) and a hopper (*see page 50*). Both pull sand out of their respective containers via siphoning action that's powered by an air compressor.

For best results, make sure the sand or other material you're using is absolutely dry. Most sandblasters have a difficult time picking up wet sand, and it has a tendency to clump up, resulting in clogs. To help prevent clogs, keep the pickup tube near the surface instead of burying it in the sand.

BLEEDER VS. NONBLEEDER SANDBLASTERS

Just as with most paint sprayers and air brushes, sandblasters are available in either bleeder or non-bleeder types. On a bleeder-type sandblaster, air passes continuously through the gun and is not controlled by the trigger. The advantage to this type of sandblaster is that it allows you to use the gun with a continuous-running tankless compressor.

Although air is supplied continuously to a nonbleeder type of sandblaster, the trigger controls the airflow through the gun. When the trigger is off, no air flows. When depressed, air flows through it and siphoning action occurs. Some sandblasters are available that can be switched back and forth between the two modes.

Using a hopper I've had better luck using a hopper with a sandblaster than using a pickup tube. This may be because the sand has less distance to travel before it enters the gun. The other reason I prefer a hopper is because of the mobility that it offers.

The only thing I don't like about a hopper is that it can be a pain to fill. I've found that a garden trowel works well for this. As you fill the hopper, be on the lookout for clumps or oversized particles that could clog up the feed line or nozzle.

Basic motion Always wear eye protection when sandblasting, and consider a dust mask, particularly when cleaning metal and masonry. Keep your hands away from the blast nozzle, as high-velocity sand will quickly remove skin, too. To help with cleanup and to protect surfaces, spread drop cloths under and around the work area.

When you're ready to blast, depress the trigger and slowly move the nozzle toward the surface to be cleaned. When the surface begins to abrade, slowly move the gun up and down, working on a 3" to 6" area at a time.

ABRASIVES FOR SANDBLASTING

Type of Abrasive	Application
Aluminum oxide grit size 50–80	Removal of rough surface paint, heavy removal of rust
Glass beads	Fine etching of glass, fine polishing of wood, silver, and brass objects
Sand grit size 30	General-purpose cleaning: light stone and cement removal, brick, glass, metal, light rust, and water deposits
Sand grit sizes 70–90	Glass etching, automotive parts cleaning and polishing, antique wood, brass, and silver polishing

A pressure washer can be a real time-saver when it comes to tough cleaning jobs, including light paint and rust removal. You can use a pressure washer with detergent to wash away grease and grime; or without, for jobs like cleaning a surface prior to painting, where soap residue could ruin a paint job.

Since you'll be directing high-pressure water at a surface where it will inevitably bounce back toward you, it's important to protect yourself and the surrounding area. Wear safety glasses or goggles and use drop cloths to cover surfaces you don't want to get wet and to allow for easy cleanup when the job is done.

Before you begin, make sure pets and children are safely out of the way. Check the nozzle for debris and remove any you find. Then, following the manufacturer's directions, turn off all valves on the pressure washer in preparation for connecting the air, water, and chemical hoses.

1 Hook up water and air To get the pressure washer ready for use, start by hooking up a garden hose to the water inlet on the pressure washer. Make sure you use the rubber washer provided, to prevent water leaks.

Then hook up your air hose to the air port on the washer. I strongly recommend using a quick-disconnect, as shown: It'll save you the hassle of pulling out an adjustable wrench every time you want to disconnect the air.

2 Applying additives To spray detergent or other chemicals, connect the draw hose supplied by the manufacturer to the pressure washer (this is usually a small, clear plastic hose). Then connect the weighted inlet to the draw hose. Now you can drop the weighted inlet into your premixed solution. Make sure that it drops to the bottom and that there are no kinks in the hose.

Quick Tip: To keep myself from getting tangled in the air, water, and draw hoses, I'll often loosely tape the hoses together with duct tape every foot or so.

Air Tools

3 Adjusting the pressure Make sure that the compressor and its electrical connections will not get wet, then adjust the regulator on the compressor to 90 psi, or to the pressure recommended by the manufacturer.

If you have any concerns about the delicacy of the surface to be sprayed, start with the pressure down around 50 psi and choose an inconspicuous spot to test. If you don't encounter any problems (*see Step 5 below*), raise the pressure to 60 psi. Continue testing and raising the pressure until you encounter problems (then back off) or until you reach 90 psi.

4 Basic operation The number one rule to using a pressure washer is: Keep the nozzle moving. Depending on the surface you're spraying, staying in one place too long can cause serious damage.

This is especially true when pressure washing the siding on a house. The high-pressure water can easily get under and lift up the siding. If you are planning on cleaning your siding, make sure to point the nozzle toward the ground as you wash. This also helps prevent water from creeping in where it doesn't belong.

5 Too much pressure Using too high a pressure is also a sure way to damage a work surface (like the siding shown). I once made the mistake of hiring a local fellow to pressure-wash an old Victorian house I owned so I could paint it. He borrowed a pressure washer from a friend and blasted my house using too high a pressure. When I drove up that night, I was dumbfounded to see dozens of scalloped moldings, gingerbread, and shingles scattered around the house. It looked like there had been a minor explosion inside the house. Don't let this happen to you—start low and slowly build up the pressure.

SANDERS

Air-powered sanders are becoming more and more popular in home workshops. They're lighter, quieter, and in many cases more powerful than their electric counterparts. Another advantage is that they're all mechanically very simple in design. This is particularly advantageous for a tool that's subjected to clouds of dust. And because they don't use electricity, you can safely use them even in wet conditions without having to worry about electric shock.

Common air-powered sanding tools are: random-orbit sanders (commonly referred to as a dual-action sander in the automotive trades), jitterbug (or orbital) sanders, and in-line (or finish) sanders.

The only disadvantage I've found to air-powered sanders is that they're air hogs. Virtually every type really gobbles up air. This means that you'll need a fairly stout compressor to run them—a unit that's capable of producing 4 to 6 cfm.

You can run air sanders on a smaller compressor, but it'll likely run almost constantly. And there's no quicker way to shorten the life of a compressor than working it beyond its capabilities.

Random-orbit Of all the air sanders out there, the random-orbit sander is my favorite. Its unique sanding pattern (*see below*) lets you sand wood with almost total disregard to grain. Because of this, random-orbit sanders are terrific for leveling joints where the grain of the parts is perpendicular (like a frame-and-panel door).

Also, these sanders chew through material fast, whether it's leveling a layer of automotive filler or smoothing a final coat of finish. Note: Always start a random-orbit sander with the disk in contact with the surface; doing otherwise can cause swirl marks.

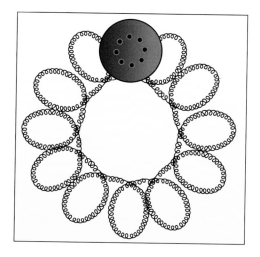

Random-orbit pattern A random-orbit sander is sort of a hybrid of a disk sander and a jitterbug sander (*see page 54*): It combines the large swirling motions of a disk sander with the smaller orbits of a jitterbug sander.

The secret to creating a random pattern has to do with an off-set cam that connects the drive motor to the sanding disk. As the disk moves over the surface, the sandpaper attached to the disk grabs the surface, causing the offset to engage and swirl the disk in a totally random pattern.

Air Tools

Jitterbug For years, jitterbug or orbital sanders were the mainstay in woodworking. They are reliable, they leave few swirl marks, and they are inexpensive. Although I do reach for a random-orbit sander for most sanding jobs, a jitterbug offers a number or advantages in some cases.

Because it's not as aggressive as a random-orbit, it's easier to use in confined spaces, and its square pad allows you to reach into corners (like inside a drawer or all the way into the back of a shelf). Their less-aggressive action also makes them ideal for delicate jobs where finesse is required.

Jitterbug pattern Although the tiny orbits of a jitterbug or orbital sander are preset by the amount of offset between the sanding pad and the motor shaft, the pattern that the sander produces depends on how fast you move the sander. The orbits are so small, you don't usually see them.

The first time I did see the orbit pattern, it was disastrous. I was smoothing the final finish on a table and came across a "clinker"—a particle on the sandpaper larger than the rest. It scratched a clearly defined pattern on the tabletop similar to that shown in the drawing.

In-line sanders An in-line sander uses a back-and-forth motion that most approximates hand sanding. The big difference is that the stroke is only about ½" long. In-line sanders (often referred to straight-line sanders) use long strips of sandpaper (typically 9" to 17") that are held in place with built-in clamps.

Although not as aggressive as random-orbit sanders, these tools provide the ultimate in smooth, flat surfaces. *Quick Tip*: If you do need to remove material fast, try holding the sander at about a 45° angle to the work surface.

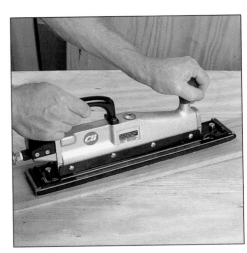

I was first introduced to air-powered drills in a production shop I worked in that manufactured high-end displays and fixtures for stores. Virtually every cabinetmaker in the shop used one of these instead of an electric drill. Curious, I borrowed one and soon learned why they were so popular.

First, because it's so much smaller and lighter-weight than an electric drill, an air-powered drill fits in the palm of your hand. Second, the better fit means better control, since you're not wrestling with the bulk and weight of an electric drill. The other thing that makes these drills so handy is that their small size lets you in to drill holes in places where larger electric drills can't get into. All of this together adds up to more precise drilling.

The air-powered drills that I first used all had keyed chucks. Since I'd become quite used to the keyless chucks on my electric drills, I felt this was a major drawback. Fortunately, nowadays most air drill manufacturers offer air drills with keyless chucks.

Basic use Once you get used to their diminutive size and lighter weight, air-powered drills operate virtually the same way as electric drills. The one difference I've noted has to do with power. If the compressor supplying the air is heavy-duty, the air drill, although small, can be quite powerful.

This is great until a drill bit catches. When this happens, the drill can "wrench" your wrist with surprising force. This can occur with any drill; it's just that when it happens with a small drill, it can startle you.

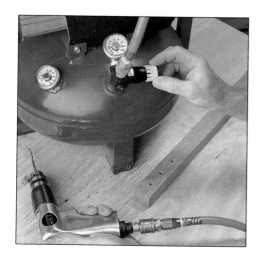

Varying speeds Some air-powered drills have built-in adjustments so that you can vary the speed. In many cases, speed is controlled by the trigger, just like an electric drill. Other models have an adjustment screw that although isn't as convenient, provides for rock-steady speed.

On drills without a variable-speed feature, you can adjust the speed somewhat by varying the pressure provided by the compressor. Note: Many drills require a minimum pressure to operate; if you adjust below this, they won't work.

IMPACT WRENCHES

I have an amateur auto mechanic neighbor who bought an air compressor just so he could use an impact wrench. Of course now that he's got air power, he uses it for almost everything. But I swear he over-maintains his vehicles just so he can use his impact wrench.

If you've ever busted your knuckles trying to work a nut loose, you'll appreciate the power and simplicity of an impact wrench. They're inexpensive and incredibly easy to use. Because of the impact involved, it's important to wear safety glasses whenever you use one; metal fragments can and do break off and go flying in the air—take the time to protect your eyes.

Since you'll most often use an impact wrench around sharp objects and metal edges, it's important to be aware of the air hose and protect it from accidental puncture. Covering metal edges with a mat or a small rug is a good way to prevent this from happening.

Changing sockets There are two common variations for attaching sockets: a detent ball or a retaining ring. Either system works fine. To attach sockets and adapters, simply push them onto the output shaft as far as they will go.

Keep in mind that it's best to keep the tool-to-socket hookup as simple as possible. Every additional connection will absorb energy and reduce power. Here again, make sure the sockets you use are labeled "for use with impact wrenches." Standard sockets aren't designed to withstand the percussion of an impact wrench.

Basic use Most impact wrenches have a built-in regulator that lets you adjust the speed and torque of the tool. Be aware that the torque numbers on the regulator are not accurate—they're just a rough indicator. If you need accurate torque, tighten the bolt by hand with a torque wrench.

An impact wrench can loosen or tighten nuts and bolts and is controlled either by a separate switch or by a two-way trigger. To prevent damage to the tool, don't change rotation direction while the trigger is on.

Changing tips The tip or point of a die grinder that actually does the grinding or sharpening is held in place by a split collet. When the nut on the end of the collet is tightened, the collet locks the shaft in place.

There are two common ways to do this. The first (*as shown here*) uses two wrenches: one to hold the motor shaft from rotating, the other to loosen or tighten the nut. With the other method, you need only a single wrench because there's a pin at the tip of the motor housing that, when depressed, keeps the shaft from rotating.

In use Since the motor speed of most die grinders is around 22,000 rpm (revolutions per minute), they can quickly remove a lot of material—sometimes more than you want. Because of this, it's important to use a gentle touch for many jobs, especially when you first begin.

Whenever possible, clamp the workpiece to keep it from moving, and use both hands to control the grinder. Turn the grinder on and ease the grinding point into the workpiece. Stop often and blow away debris so you can check your progress.

GRINDING TIP TYPES

There is a wide variety of tips and grinding points available for a die grinder. The assortment shown here illustrates just a few of the various sizes and abrasive grits out there.

In addition to grinding points, you can also purchase cutting burrs and mills that are extremely useful for woodcarving and sculpting. Grinding points and tips typically come with either ⅛" or ¼" shafts—many die grinders come with collets to accept both sizes.

BLOW GUNS

Of all the air tools I own, the one I reach for most often is the smallest and the simplest—the blow gun. Because I do a lot of woodworking, I'm always using it to blow sawdust out of a freshly drilled hole, clear out dust inside a drawer after sanding, or quickly clean off the top of my table saw.

A blow gun is also extremely useful for cleaning tools and equipment that have lots of crevices that can trap dirt and dust.

But a blow gun has many more uses than simply propelling dust off a surface. Fitted with an assortment of nozzles (*see below*), a blow gun can inflate a variety of sports and leisure equipment, including bicycle and automobile tires.

Whatever type of inflator nozzle you use, make sure to check the inflatable object for recommended pressure and adjust your compressor accordingly (*see page 59* for more on this).

Nozzle types Although I keep a rubber-tipped safety nozzle on my blow gun most of the time, I use the other nozzle types on a regular basis. *Shown here from top to bottom:* a pressure gauge; a chuck for inflating tires; the main nozzle body with trigger; a needle for filling up sports equipment, pool toys, etc.; and a barbed general-purpose inflator tool that can usually fill up anything with air that doesn't accept one of the other nozzles. All of these tips have threads on one end that screw into the business end of the blow gun. (Also shown are various quick-connect fittings.)

Basic use Regardless of what nozzle you'll be using, apply a drop or two of oil to the threads of the nozzle before screwing it into the blow gun, to make it easy to change it in the future. I generally don't use Teflon tape here, because I often change nozzles and I don't need a perfect seal.

If you're using the blow gun to clean off a surface, keep the gun about 8" to 10" away and squeeze the trigger in short bursts. This helps prevent dust from circulating around the shop.

Adjust pressure The most important aspect to using any blow gun nozzle or tire chuck is to match the air pressure coming from the compressor to the job at hand.

As a general rule of thumb, use a low pressure (around 40 to 50 psi) to start with, and then increase it if necessary. It's always safer to take a little longer to inflate something with a lower pressure than to run the risk of bursting it with a blast of high pressure.

Inflator tip The most delicate nozzle tip for the blow gun is the inflator tip. Whenever you use this tip, take great care to keep the blow gun as still as possible once the tip has been inserted. The combined weight of the blow gun and the air hose can easily provide sufficient force to snap the tip off if moved just a little during filling.

Having snapped off plenty of tips myself (due to excited kids accidentally tripping on the air hose), I've learned to gently step on the hose a couple of feet back from the blow gun to provide strain relief.

Lubricate tip When you do go to use an inflator tip, take the time to put a drop of oil or dish soap (*as shown*) onto the tip before inserting it. This can dramatically increase the life of the inflatable object by not only easing the insertion, but also keeping the inflator valve lubricated. A well-lubricated air valve will have less of a tendency to dry out and crack over time, so it will be less likely to develop leaks.

4 ADVANCED OPERATIONS

Two of the most common advanced operations for which many homeowners purchase air compressors are applying paint and finishes with a spray gun and driving fasteners with an air nailer.

The benefits of spraying paint and finishes are many. First and foremost, spraying is fast. You can apply multiple coats of lacquer to a bookcase or spraypaint a single-level house in a day. Second, you can spray almost anything from contact cement for new laminate to a fresh coat of stain for a deck.

Spray finishes are more forgiving than brushed-on finishes because they can be applied in lighter coats that tend to hide scratches and surface blemishes.

Air nailers, from heavy-duty framing nailers to the smallest brad nailer, give everyone the ability to drive fasteners like a seasoned pro. A pull of the trigger is all it takes to drive and set a fastener in the blink of an eye. But there's a catch. Because they're so powerful, you'll need to learn and follow a set of safety rules to prevent accidents from happening.

In this chapter, I'll start by taking you through everything you need to know to successfully apply a sprayed-on finish. I'll begin by going over how to prepare both your work area and the object to be sprayed. Then we'll move on to setting up and filling the spray gun, and finally spraying on the finish (*see pages 61–65*).

The second half of the chapter is devoted to air nailers. I'll begin with the industrial-strength version—the framing nailer (*pages 66–67 and 70*).

A very important section, which pertains to all air-powered fastening tools, is next: fastening safety (*pages 68–69*). I can't over-emphasize the importance of developing good safety habits when working with one of these tools. Although many of the rules seem like common sense, nailer accidents continue to occur at an alarming level.

The rest of this section is devoted to reviewing the operation and use of finish nailers, narrow crown staplers, and finally, brad nailers (*pages 71, 72, and 73, respectively*).

SPRAYING PAINT AND FINISHES

The first thing you should know about spraying on paint or finish is the time devoted to actually spraying can be a small portion of the overall job. The bulk of your time will be devoted to preparing to spray (*see below*) and then cleaning up afterwards (*see pages 94–97* for more on cleaning and lubricating a spray gun).

In terms of preparation, you'll first need to select a place to spray. For most of us, this means the basement, garage, workshop, or outdoors. The primary requirement of any location is adequate ventilation.

With this in mind, I don't recommend spraying in a basement. Besides the circulation problem, a water heater or furnace kicking on can spark an explosion if a flammable material is being sprayed.

Stick with the garage, workshop, or outdoors. If you're inside, set up fans to pull in fresh air and exhaust the old air, and always wear a paint-spray or organic-vapor respirator to protect your lungs. For outdoor jobs, make sure the conditions match those specified by the manufacturers—for both temperature and humidity.

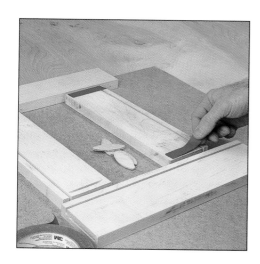

1 Surface preparation The first thing to do before you even open a can of paint or finish is to prepare the surface you're about to spray. Start by removing all dust, dirt, or loose particles. If you're spraying in the same room where you've been building the project, let the dust settle and then vacuum the project and work area thoroughly.

On some jobs, you may want to mask off areas before spraying. In the example shown, I'm covering areas of drawer parts to be glued up—any finish here would interfere with the glue bond.

2 Area preparation Regardless of the finish you're applying, spraying always generates a fine mist. To prevent this from covering your shop and coating your lungs, you need to set up an appropriate area to spray. If the object you're spraying is small, you can set up a simple spray booth with a scrap of plywood on a pair of sawhorses.

A prefolded "science fair" display board (*as shown here*) is available at office supply stores and works great for a temporary backdrop. Covering an ordinary floor fan with a filter will help draw the finish away from you and your shop.

3 **Check viscosity** Although many finishes can be sprayed right from the can, there are times when you'll need to thin the finish in order to get a smooth, even finish. Most manufacturers provide thinning recommendations right on the can. Some spray gun manufacturers will indicate how thin a material should be for a specific needle/tip combination.

You can measure the thickness of a material, or "viscosity," with a viscosity cup. Timing how long it takes for the material to drain from the cup indicates its viscosity and whether it should be thinned or not (*see the chart below*).

4 **Strain finish** Cleanliness is extremely important in spraying, since even the smallest particle of dust or dirt can ruin a job. You've cleaned the work area and project, but how about the finish? Even if you've just opened a fresh can, odds are there are impurities in it; cans that have been previously opened will undoubtedly collect dust and dirt.

To prevent impurities from affecting your finish, take the time to strain the material before filling the spray canister. A disposable paper filter like the one shown makes this a quick and easy task. Disposable paint filters are available at most hardware stores, paint stores, and home centers.

TYPICAL VISCOSITY TIMES FOR COMMON MATERIALS

Material	enamel	exterior oil-based paint	exterior latex paint	interior latex paint	lacquer	varnish
Time (in seconds)	30	35	35	35	20	25

5 Fill canister When you're spraying only a small amount, you can combine the straining and filling by inserting the strainer into the canister and then filling. For larger spray quantities, it's best to strain into another container—especially if you're using multiple cans of paint—this way you can intermix cans to even out the color.

To save yourself cleanup time when the job is done, many spray gun manufacturers sell disposable plastic liners that fit inside the canister and are held in place when the lid is attached.

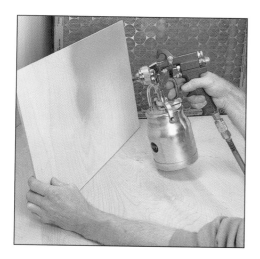

6 Spray test pattern Once the canister is filled, attach the air hose and adjust the compressor pressure according the spray gun manufacturer's directions to match the type of finish you're spraying.

Then, holding the gun about 8" to 12" away from a scrap of cardboard or plywood, give the trigger a quick pull to spray a test pattern. If the material sputters, odds are that it's too thick and needs to be thinned. If the spray pattern isn't equal, see *pages 112–113*.

SPRAY PATTERNS

The pattern a spray gun creates will depend on the type of air cap used. The two most common air cap patterns available are fan and round. For a variety of spray patterns, some advanced spray guns have a pattern control knob above the fluid adjustment.

Fan pattern: A fan pattern is particularly suited for spraying flat, wide surfaces, such as a tabletop.

Round pattern: A round pattern is best for general-purpose spraying and small, irregular-shaped work.

7 Adjust spray gun On most spray guns, there are two controls that need adjusting to create a solid, even pattern. Start by adjusting the fluid control to get good material flow. Then adjust the pressure of the fluid as it flows to the tip by adjusting the air control knob.

Getting the proper material flow can be tricky and will likely require some trial and error. But as long as the material's viscosity and the incoming air pressure are correct, this shouldn't take too long.

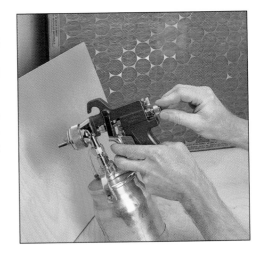

8 Basic technique If you've never sprayed before, take some time to practice correct spraying technique. Start by holding the gun 8" to 12" from the surface. Depress the trigger, and begin the stroke. Keep the gun moving in a straight line, parallel to and an even distance away from the surface, as shown in the bottom half of the drawing.

Make sure the tip of the gun is also parallel to the surface. A common mistake is to move the gun in an arc, as shown in the top half of the drawing; doing so will lay down an uneven pattern—too much material in the center and not enough at the edges.

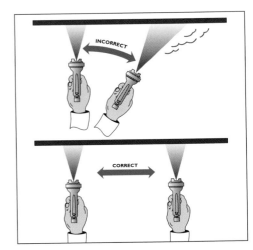

9 Overlapping strokes To reduce the likelihood of thin spots and to guarantee even coverage, each pass that you make with the spray gun should overlap the previous stroke by about half.

On large, flat surfaces, like tabletops or walls, you'll achieve more consistent coverage by making two lighter passes in opposite directions than by making a single heavy pass.

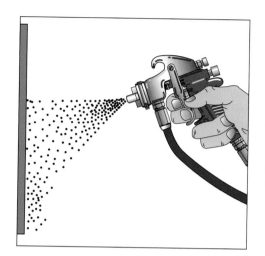

10 **No tilt** Just as moving the spray gun in an arc will create an uneven pattern, tilting the spray gun at an angle will also cause problems. When the tip of the gun is not parallel to the work surface (*as shown*), the material being sprayed will lay down heavier on either the top or the bottom, depending on which way the gun is tilted. This often results in sagging or runs.

Quick Tip: If you're having problems keeping the gun level, consider attaching a small bubble level to the gun as a visual reference.

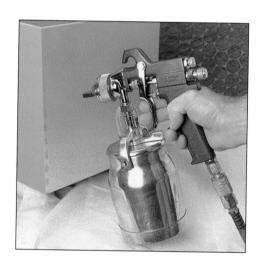

11 **Setup and follow-through** Just as with a good golf or baseball swing, setup and follow-through are important parts of good spraying technique. To get the most consistent results, start your stroke 6" to 8" in front of the surface. Depress the trigger and move the gun steadily across the surface.

When you reach the end of the surface, don't stop. Instead, continue moving and spraying for another 6" to 8" past the edge. Although this does create a small amount of overspray, you'll enjoy complete, even coverage from edge to edge.

12 **Detail guns** A detail gun is used much like a standard spray gun. The big difference is that you can get into tighter spaces because the gun is smaller, lighter, and easier to maneuver. On most detail sprayers, the trigger is on top of the gun and is usually depressed with the thumb, as shown.

I find that holding the sprayer like this, combined with the lighter weight of the gun, allows my wrist to be more flexible, allowing for tighter control and more fluid movements.

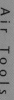

FRAMING NAILERS

The first thing you'll notice about using a framing nailer is the size and weight of the nailer itself—these guys are big and heavy. A framing nailer without a hose will typically run between 8 and 12 pounds.

Add another couple pounds for the hose and fasteners, and you could easily be toting around 15 pounds. With this in mind, the balance of the tool is very important, and the type of hose that you use can tip the balance scale one way or the other.

If you discover that the tool is awkward to handle, consider a lighter or heavier hose. A hose can serve as a counterbalance, much like the long pole that a tightrope walker uses. For a heavier air hose, try a hose designed for use with hydraulics. They're more than capable of handling the pressure and are very rugged. If you need a lighter hose, try the clear plastic variety as shown on *page 24.*

Toenail Without a doubt, the ability to toenail a wall stud in perfect position with the pull of a trigger is what sold me on framing nailers. Holding the gun at the proper angle, press the nosepiece firmly into the workpiece until the spiked tip grabs hold, and then continue pressing to engage the safety mechanism.

Pull the trigger to drive the nail. Since a nailer drives the nail in the blink of an eye, you'll find that you don't need a death grip on the workpiece to hold it in position.

Flush-nail Flush-nailing with a framing nailer is simplicity itself. Here again, just press and shoot. Since shooting nails is so easy with a framing nailer, one thing to watch out for is overnailing. This is particularly critical when nailing near the end of a workpiece. Excessive nails here can and will cause the end of the workpiece to split (*see page 123* for more on splitting).

Spiked tip The tips on most framing nailers are spiked like the one shown. This allows you to jab the nosepiece firmly into a workpiece so the spikes can penetrate into it and prevent the nailer from sliding around.

The size and number of the spikes or teeth will determine how aggressively the tip will grab a workpiece. If you use your nailer a lot, the teeth will eventually dull and lose their ability to grip. A couple of strokes to each tooth with a small triangular mill file will bring back the sharp points.

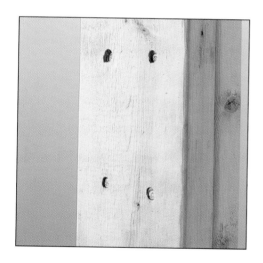

Stair-stepped nails Stair-stepped nails or "staircasing" is a sure sign that the compressor you're using doesn't have enough punch. Basically, the nailer isn't getting sufficient air to drive nails to a consistent depth, as shown.

A more common example of this is when the nails stand proud of the workpiece; the first fastener will be driven all the way in, the next will be a little higher, and the next even higher. The best solution is to use a compressor with a cfm to match the nailer. If this isn't possible, slow down to let the compressor fill the tank to sufficient pressure.

DEPTH ADJUSTMENT

With most nailers, you have to fiddle around with the compressor pressure to get the nailer to shoot a nail and set it the correct depth. This can be a real pain if the compressor is on the ground and you're up on a ladder or on a roof.

A nice feature on some high-quality nailers is a built-in depth adjustment, fitted into the nose like the one shown. A turn of the knob or a thumbwheel is all it takes to adjust the depth to the desired setting.

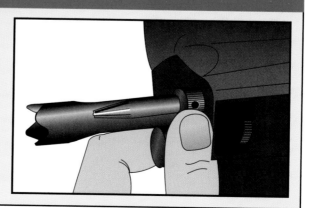

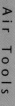

FASTENING SAFETY

Just like any power tool, an air-powered nailer can be dangerous, even fatal, if it is used improperly. The secret to preventing accidents is learning and following the safety rules for the tool. Some of the safety precautions I'll discuss here I'm sure will seem like common sense. But the number of air-nailer accidents that continue to happen on a daily basis indicates that common sense is being ignored.

If you start practicing safe tool handling and nailing technique now, it'll quickly develop into habit. And the few extra seconds these steps take can save you or someone else from a serious injury.

Make sure that you take the time to read and follow the safety precautions described in the air-powered nailer's user manual. It's also a good idea to check the safety mechanism of the nailer on a regular basis; if doesn't work properly, take it in to a service center immediately for repair.

Wear glasses The number one safety rule for using an air nailer is to wear safety glasses—every time you pick up the gun, get in the habit of checking to make sure you've got them on. Most manufacturers include a pair with the air nailer.

Since air nailers often cause fragments or fasteners to ricochet at odd angles, anyone working in your immediate area should also have safety glasses on as well. Safety glasses not only protect your eyes from fragments, but also protect them from the burst of air or exhaust from the nailer.

Hose clearance Air hoses often cause accidents. First off, if the hose gets tangled around your feet, you can trip and fall. Second, if you're carrying an air nailer when you trip, you'll damage the nailer, or more importantly, you could accidentally fire a fastener into something or someone (including yourself).

The simplest way to prevent this is to be aware of the hose at all times; keep excess hose coiled away from your feet. Some types of hose, like the plastic one shown here, have a tendency to not lie flat. Be especially careful when working with these.

Disconnect before reloading or servicing If there's one safety rule that I constantly see being ignored, it's loading a magazine or clearing a jam without first disconnecting the air hose. This is like trying to clean a handgun while it's loaded—it's just a matter of time before someone gets hurt.

Disconnecting the air hose takes one, maybe two seconds. Take the time to do this—you'll be glad you did. Note: Because it's self-sealing, never install a female quick-connect on a nailer—the gun can remain pressurized even after you've disconnected the hose.

Don't carry with trigger depressed Probably the number one cause of serious nailer injuries is caused by carrying a nailer set up for "bounce" firing with the trigger depressed. As long as the trigger is depressed, the nailer will shoot a fastener whenever the safety mechanism or contact point is depressed. The nailer can't tell the difference between a 2×4 and your knee.

Again, I'm sure this seems obvious, but I've caught myself doing it when laying roofing shingles. To prevent this, don't just release the trigger—remove your finger completely, as shown.

Don't point gun toward yourself I can't tell you how many times I've seen someone point a nailer at themselves as in the photo. In every case when I've pointed out what they were doing, they stepped back, shook their head, and turned red.

If you work with air nailers a lot, it's easy to become complacent. I often suggest to folks that they use the same mindset for handling an air nailer that they'd use for handling a weapon—although air nailers don't have the range of a handgun, they are just as dangerous.

FRAMING-NAILER OPERATION

Basic use The type of firing system your framing nailer uses, either sequential or touch-trip (*see below*), will determine how it will shoot fasteners. With either system, the safety mechanism has to be engaged first.

Just press the nosepiece of the nailer into the workpiece until the safety mechanism engages. If the nailer is a touch-trip and the trigger is depressed, it'll shoot a fastener. On a sequential-trip nailer, depress the trigger to shoot a fastener.

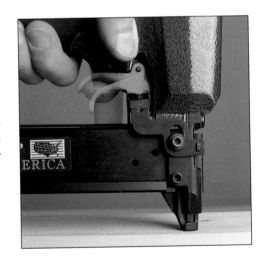

Sequential firing Framing nailers with sequential firing systems require you to pull the trigger each time you want to shoot a fastener, once the safety mechanism has been engaged.

In addition to pulling the trigger each time, a restricted sequential system requires you to lift up the gun to reset the safety mechanism after every fastener is shot. This differs from standard sequential, where you can depress the safety mechanism and slide the gun along, shooting fasteners every time the trigger is pulled.

Touch-trip or "bounce" firing Touch-trip or bounce-firing systems allow you to hold the trigger down and shoot a fastener every time the contact point or safety mechanism is depressed. Although this does allow for rapid firing of fasteners, it also is the most dangerous way to shoot fasteners.

I found that sequential firing took a bit of getting used to; but once I got used to it, I found I could shoot fasteners at almost the same speed as with a touch trip—but much more safely.

In many situations where you're using a finish nailer, you'll be pressing a part against a wall or ceiling or you'll be pressing two parts together. To get the best fastener penetration when working against a wall or ceiling that's not plumb or level, insert shims as needed to support the part; when pressing two parts together, support them on something sturdy like a stout table or workbench.

Although finish nailers shoot smaller fasteners than their larger framing-nailer cousins, you'll still need to take similar safety precautions (*see pages 68–69*) when shooting fasteners. Also, it's important to have the correct compressor pressure in order to drive the fasteners to the correct depth. Check your owner's manual for recommended settings.

Attach trim A finish nailer excels at attaching trim. Just hold the trim piece in place, press the nosepiece into it, and pull the trigger. Faster than you can blink, it'll secure the trim.

If by chance the trim isn't exactly where you want it, don't try to dig out the nail. Instead, pull the trim piece off with a pair of pliers and then pull the nail out through the back of the trim piece. Don't be tempted to drive the brad out from behind with a hammer: The square head of the nail when driven backwards will inevitably split the wood.

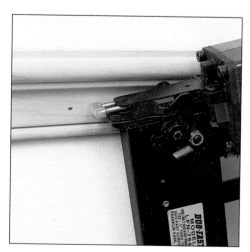

No-mar tip The tip you use with a finish nailer will have a lot to do with how well it works. I've had best luck with a rubber tip, like the one shown here. Larger cushion tips are available; but they're usually round, and I find that they don't fit into crevices nearly as well as the small, rectangular rubber ones.

The only disadvantage to the rubber tips is they do get chewed up with use. So I'd recommend keeping a replacement tip or two on hand for emergencies.

Air Tools

NARROW CROWN STAPLERS

Stapling backs When it comes to using a narrow crown stapler, one thing that's different from other nailers is the precautions you have to take because of the size of the staple you're shooting. Since staples can be much larger than brads, or even finish nails, you have to be careful where you shoot them, as they have a tendency to split wood; *see below*.

The other thing you'll discover about using a narrow crown stapler is, since it's driving two points into a workpiece instead of one, it often requires greater cfm (greater airflow) than a small finish nailer or brad nailer.

Adding glue blocks The added grip that staples offer over nails and brads make them particularly useful for situations where parts will be stressed. The glue blocks shown here are a good example of this.

Glue blocks like this are often used to provide support to table legs and chair legs. The large indentation that a staple leaves isn't a problem when it won't be seen.

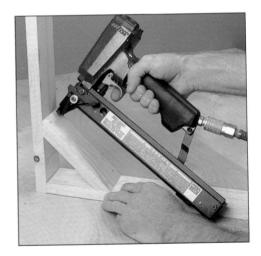

Grain orientation Lighter-gauge staples (especially long ones) have a tendency to follow the grain when shot into hardwood. As the point of the staple drives into the wood, it is easily deflected when it hits a growth ring. When this happens, the staple takes the path of least resistance and, depending on the workpiece, can even shoot out of the side (*as shown*).

This rarely happens in softer wood. Following the grain also leads to splitting. This is especially true near the edge of a workpiece. Orienting the staple perpendicular to the grain can help prevent this from happening.

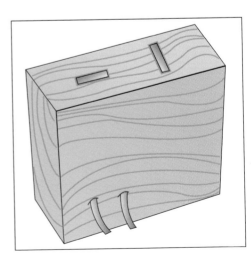

Invisible fastening One of the biggest advantages a brad nailer offers over a conventional hammer and nail set is not only does it drive and countersink the brad in one quick motion, but it also leaves an almost invisible indentation.

This is particularly useful when applying edging to cover the raw edge of plywood (*as shown*) or when installing decorative trim where you don't want the fastener to show. Just a tiny amount of wood putty will cover the indentation.

Push and shoot Press the nosepiece of the brad nailer into the workpiece to disengage the safety mechanism. Pull the trigger to shoot a fastener. On brad nailers with a double trigger, there is no safety mechanism in the nosepiece. Instead, you pull one trigger and then the other to shoot a fastener (in either order).

Caution: Since brads are smaller-gauge then other fasteners, they're easily deflected by wood grain—if you're using one hand to hold the workpiece in place, make sure to keep that hand a safe distance from the nailer.

DIFFERENT BRAD-NAILER TIPS

There are a number of tips available for brad nailers. The most common, a bent metal tip like the left nailer shown, has a tendency to mar the workpiece.

Some manufacturers offer a cushion tip or a high-impact plastic tip (*at right in photo*) that offer better protection from marring.

Quick Tip: I've found applying a layer or two of duct tape temporarily to the end of the metal tip will prevent scratches and dings on delicate or soft surfaces.

Air Tools

SHOP-MADE JIGS FOR AIR TOOLS

There are three common reasons people build jigs and fixtures for tools. First, they don't want to pay the price of a commercially available version. Second, many times they can't find the features they're looking for in the store-bought jigs that are available. And third, often there just is no equivalent jig or fixture available on the market. Sometimes you just can't find a jig that does what you need it to do. I build jigs for these reasons and more. I like solving problems and the challenge of designing a "better" mousetrap.

In this chapter I've designed four jigs that will help you get more out of your air tools. The first project—the Wall-Mounted Air Station *on page 75*—falls under the "there just isn't anything like this out there" umbrella. I needed a simple system to store and organize my air tools and accessories while keeping them handy. I just couldn't find anything except cabinets. A cabinet would work fine for storage, but what about an air hose? Or a filter/regulator? What I came up with is a wall-mounted system that's modular; that is, you can move holders around to fit your changing needs.

The second jig—a portable hose —is one of those "I just can't see paying that much for..." scenarios. Here again, I was looking for something that would allow me to store and organize accessories, but this time for a portable compressor. Really, just something to keep the air hose from underfoot and maybe hold a tool or two. The solution is simple and effective; *see page 78.*

Jig number three is a sturdy case to protect a brad nailer, finish nailer, narrow crown stapler, or whatever type of air nailer you have. If your nailer doesn't have a case, or if the case it came with is cheap (or if it doesn't have the features you want, like built-in storage for nails and other such items), consider building a rugged case that looks as good as it protects. This simple project is made even easier with a nifty construction trick; *see page 80.*

The fourth jig is another case of "I'm not paying that much for a..." It's a shop-made version of a commercially available hose reel. A great way to keep your air hose from getting underfoot, keeping it tangle-free and protected from abuse. Granted, the version I designed isn't as fancy as the store-bought kind, but it gets the job done at a fraction of the cost.

Regardless of what jig you build, take the time to apply a finish to protect your investment in time and materials. A couple of coats of varnish or paint will keep a jig free from dirt while sealing it against moisture. This not only makes it look better, but will also help it last for years.

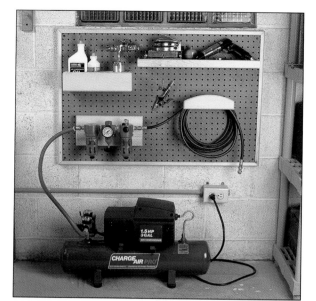

WALL-MOUNTED AIR STATION

Just like any versatile tool, an air compressor will quickly accumulate a cluster of accessories. The perpetual problem everyone faces in the shop is storing accessories like this so they're well organized yet still handy. That's where this wall-mounted air station comes in. Its modular design allows you to customize it to fit your accessories. A simple L-hook mounting system (*see page 77*) makes it easy to move holders around to fit your changing needs. And it's easily expandable in the future—just make additional holders as you add accessories. I've included directions for four common holders on *pages 76–77:* a hose holder; a shelf for tools; a box for oil, parts, and so forth; and a bracket for attaching a regulator/filter.

The foundation of the wall station is a framed piece of ¼" pegboard. The frame provides the necessary clearance between the wall and the pegboard for the hooks. Start by cutting a ¼"-deep groove in each frame piece to capture the pegboard. Miter the ends of the frame pieces, and glue the pegboard in place. Then pin the miters with brads. To provide additional support, I added glue blocks to the back of the inside corners of the frame.

PARTS LIST

Quantity	Part	Dimentions	Material
2	Station top/bottom	¾" × 1¼" × 37"	pine
2	Station sides	¾" × 1¼" × 25"	pine
1	Station pegboard	¼" × 24" × 30"	pegboard
4	Station glue blocks	¾" × 2" × 2"	pine
1	Hose bracket	1½" × 3½" × 6"	pine
1	Hose retainer	¾" × 2¾" × 9"	pine
1	Shelf	¾" × 4" × 20½"	pine
1	Shelf front lip	⅜" × 1¼" × 21¼"	pine
2	Shelf side lips	⅜" × 1¼" × 4⅜"	pine
2	Box front/back	¾" × 3¼" × 12"	pine
2	Box sides	¾" × 3¼" × 4"	pine
1	Box bottom	⅛" × 3" × 11"	hardboard
1	Regulator base	1½" × 3½" × 12"	pine
8	L-hooks	⅛" × 1¾"	metal

EXPLODED VIEW

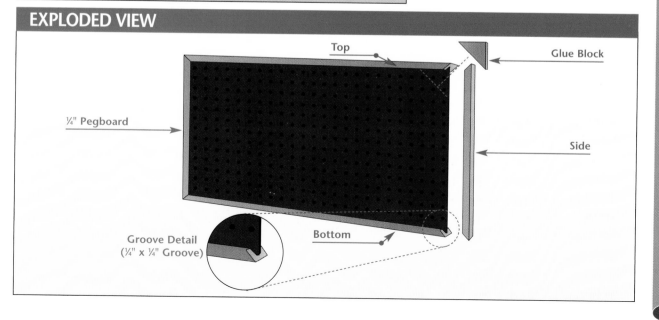

Top

Glue Block

¼" Pegboard

Side

Groove Detail
(¼" x ¼" Groove)

Bottom

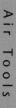

Hose holder Here's an easy-to-make holder that'll get your tangled air hose off the floor and store it safely out of harm's way. The hose holder consists of two parts: a bracket and a retainer.

The bracket is just a piece of 2×4 that's shaped in a gradual curve with its edges softened to keep from abrading the hose. The retainer attaches to the bracket with glue and nails (or screws) and prevents the hose from slipping off. Here again, it's shaped in a gradual curve and the edges are softened. A pair of L-hooks let you to attach the holder to the frame; *see the side-bar on page 77* for mounting details.

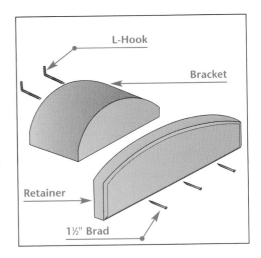

Shelf Although I designed this shelf to temporarily store tools I was using on a current project, I've noticed that the tools I use most often have ended up there permanently. (With this in mind, you may want to make more than one of these.) The shelf is a piece of pine with a lip around it to keep things from sliding off. I just glued and stapled the lips in place, then filled the indentations with wood putty.

Notice that the back top corners of the lips on the sides are mitered at 45° so you can tilt the shelf up to engage the L-hooks in the pegboard. (*See page 77* for mounting details.)

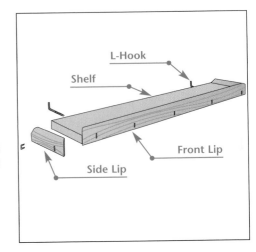

Box I don't know about you, but it's the little parts that I have trouble finding when I need them—stuff like spare couplings and nozzles. That's what this box is for. It's also a handy place to store tool oil, cleaning supplies, even small tools (like a detail sprayer or a die grinder).

The box consists of a front, a back, and two sides (all with mitered ends) and a ⅛"-thick hardboard bottom. The bottom fits in a groove cut in the bottom inside edge of each box part. I glued the box together and fastened the corners with staples. (*See page 77* for L-hook mounting details.)

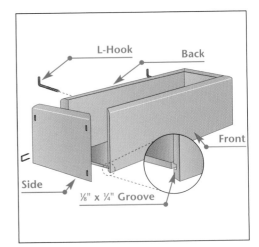

Attach frame to wall In addition to strengthening the frame, the glue blocks that are attached to the corners in back of the frame also serve another purpose: They provide a solid backing for attaching the frame to a wall. Screwing the frame to a wall without the blocks will cause the pegboard to bow in and break. The glue blocks prevent this.

To attach the frame, drill through the pegboard about ½" in from each corner and through each glue block. Then screw the frame to the wall. Use wall anchors as necessary, or if you're going into masonry as shown here, use concrete screws.

Attach regulator to base Although you might be tempted to simply screw your regulator/filter assembly directly to the pegboard, I suggest you attach it to a base with L-hooks. This keeps it modular and allows you to move it around as necessary.

The base is a piece of 2×6 with L-hooks in the back. Attach the filter/regulator assembly to the base with a pair of stout screws, as shown.

L-HOOK MOUNTING SYSTEM

The key to this pegboard system is L-hooks that screw into the back of each holder. For this to work, the L-hooks must be precisely located. First, the L-hooks must be centered on holes in the pegboard. The easiest way to do this is to butt the holder up against the pegboard and make marks centered on the holes near opposite ends. Then drill pilot holes ½" down from top edge and centered on the thickness of the part you're drilling into. Next, screw the L-hook in until there's a ⁵⁄₁₆" gap between the L portion of the hook and the back of the holder. Attach the holder to the pegboard and check the fit. If it's too loose or tight, adjust the hook in or out.

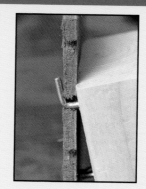
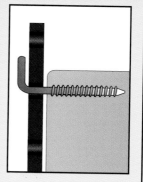

AIR-HOSE CADDY

Simple design One of features of air compressors that I like best—their portability—also creates a problem. Where do you store all the accessories when you move to a job site? In most cases, this involves multiple trips. But not if you've made this handy strap-on caddy that conveniently holds an air hose and a tool or two.

I kept the design simple on this so that you could easily modify dimensions to fit your compressor. On some handled compressors, you can lengthen the caddy so it spans across the handles. In either case, the hose caddy quickly attaches to the compressor via a pair of U-bolts.

Assemble the parts There are three parts to the portable hose caddy: two plywood sides and a 2×4 spacer. I removed the sharp corners on the sides to make it easier to wind up the air hose. It's also a good idea to relieve the corners of the spacer to keep them from abrading the hose when it's stored.

Center a side on the spacer, from top-to-bottom and from side-to-side, and attach it with glue and 1½" drywall screws. Repeat for the other side.

Attach to compressor Drill a pair of 5⁄16" holes 1" down from the top and bottom edge of one side for the U-bolts. Center these holes 1½" apart on the length of the sides. Then slip U-bolts though each set of holes, and position the hose caddy on the compressor. Slide the U-bolt plate over the threads of the bolts, thread on the nuts, and tighten.

Depending on the size of your handle, the threads of the U-bolts may protrude too far. If they do, cut them off with a hacksaw and files the edges smooth. You may want to thread on protective rubber caps to further protect the hose.

Add hooks to hold accessories The exposed face of the hose caddy presents an opportunity for storage. There are a number of options here. You could attach a small shelf or box (similar to those shown on the air station on *page 75*).

Or, as shown here, by judiciously placing a couple of L-hooks, you can easily store a brad nailer or other small tool. In most cases, all that's required is one hook to hang the tool on and another to prevent it from shifting when the compressor is carried.

PARTS LIST

Quantity	Part	Dimensions	Material
2	Sides	¾" × 10" × 12"	plywood
1	Spacer	1½" × 3½" × 6"	pine
2	U-bolts, with nuts & plate	¼" × 1¾"	metal

EXPLODED VIEW

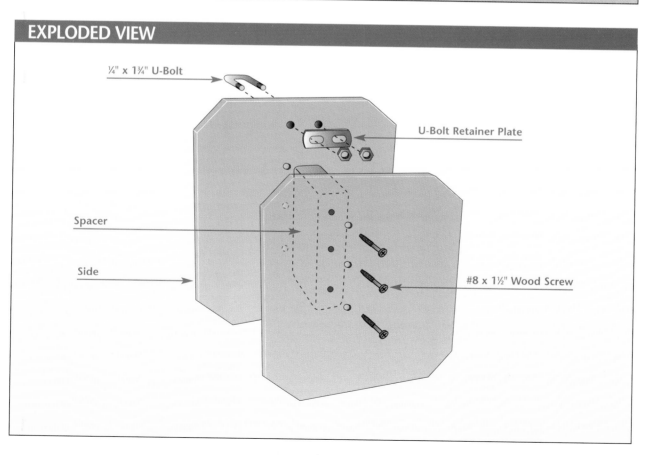

¼" x 1¾" U-Bolt

U-Bolt Retainer Plate

Spacer

Side

#8 x 1½" Wood Screw

AIR-NAILER CASE

Although some nail guns come with a case, many don't. And with the ones that do, the case is often so poorly made that it offers little protection. With the cost of a quality nail gun running anywhere from $150 to $600, it's worth the time and effort to protect your investment by building a sturdy case.

This case features a ¾"-thick hardwood frame (I used birch) and a matching plywood top and bottom. The gun itself is protected within, with inexpensive blue foam pads custom-cut to cradle the gun. I used a simple dado-and-rabbet joint to hold the case together; see the joinery detail in the Exploded View.

Cut box apart Instead of making a separate case top and bottom, I built a sealed box, then cut it in two on the table saw. Start by cutting the pieces to size (modify the dimensions as needed) and cut the joinery on the ends. Then cut or rout a groove for the plywood top and bottom.

After you've glued up the case, attach a tall auxiliary fence to your rip fence. Then set the fence 1¼" from the blade and make a pass on each end of the case. Next insert and tape ⅛"-thick shims into the kerfs (to prevent the lid from closing on the blade once it's separated), and separate the lid by cutting through the front and back.

Trace around foam Foam board is available at most lumber stores and home centers in a few thicknesses, typically ½", ¾", 1", and 1½". What you're after here is a combination that will fill most of space within the case.

I fitted a 1½" piece in the lid and a ½" and two 1" pieces in the bottom—each cut to fit snugly in the case. The two 1" pieces in the bottom will be cut to fit around the gun. To do this, start by placing the gun on the foam and trace around it with a felt-tip marker.

Cut the foam Now you can cut the foam to create the cavity for the gun. There are various tools you can use for this: a utility knife (but you'll find the blade may not be long enough, and it's difficult to go around corners) or, as shown here, a drywall saw. Its narrow tapered blade makes it easy to push through the foam to start the cut, and it can navigate the corners with ease. Or, if you've got one available, a scroll saw with a fine blade will cut through this stuff like butter and leave a nice smooth edge.

PARTS LIST

Quantity	Part	Dimensions	Material
2	Front/back	¾" × 5¼" × 17"	hardwood
2	Sides	¾" × 5¼" × 14"	hardwood
2	Top/bottom	¼" × 13⅛" × 17"	hardwood
3*	Foam inserts	¾" × 12½" × 16¼"	foam board
2	Hinges	1½" × 1½"	metal
2	Latches	1⅜" × 2¼"	metal
1	Handle	1½" × 5¾"	metal

* Quantity and thickness of foam inserts will depend on the size of your nail gun.

EXPLODED VIEW

Note:
⅜" Roundover on All Edges

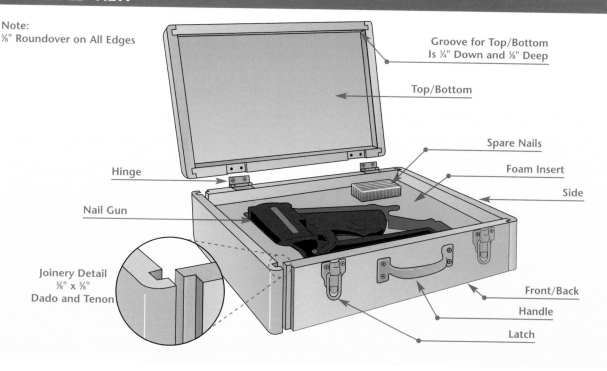

Groove for Top/Bottom Is ¼" Down and ⅜" Deep

Top/Bottom

Spare Nails

Foam Insert

Side

Hinge

Nail Gun

Joinery Detail
⅜" x ⅜"
Dado and Tenon

Front/Back

Handle

Latch

AIR-HOSE REEL

I've always liked the idea of a roll-up reel for an air hose. You pull out just the hose you need, and when you're done, a spin or two of the handle reels it in. No more tangled hose. Unfortunately, the cost of a manufactured hose reel (typically around $100) has kept me away. So I decided it was time to make one myself.

The design I came up with isn't as fancy as a store-bought version (you have to disconnect the hose from the compressor before rewinding); but it cost me less than ten bucks, and it offers built-in storage (see the Exploded View on *page 83*).

Build spool The spool that holds the air hose is made up of two 11¾"-diameter plywood circles and eight lengths of ½" dowel. You can cut the circles out with a saber saw or router with trammel point, by hand, or with a circle-cutting jig.

Then, lay out and drill eight ⅜"-deep holes for the dowels 3" out from the center. Cut the dowels to length, apply glue to one end of each dowel, and tap them into the holes on one side. Then apply glue sparingly into the holes on the other half of the spool, and press the dowels into the matching holes.

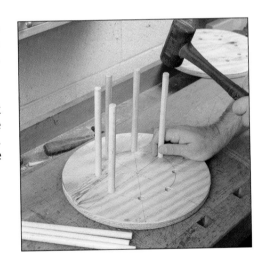

Lazy Susan The heart of the hose reel is a lazy Susan bearing. Position it on the spool and mark the mounting-hole locations. Then remove it and drill ¼" mounting holes. Attach the lazy Susan with ¼" carriage bolts, lock washers, and nuts. Next, position the spool on the support bracket, mark holes for the lazy Susan, and drill. Here again, attach it with carriage bolts.

Now you can assemble the bracket back, side, and support together with 2" drywall screws. (Note: The rabbet that runs along the edge of the bracket back aids alignment; however, a butt joint would suffice.)

Shop-Made Jigs for Air Tools

Handle All that's left is to add a simple shop-made handle. A short length of dowel and a bolt will do the job. Start by drilling a ⁷⁄₁₆" hole through the length of a 1"-diameter dowel. Then mark and drill a ⅜"-diameter hole 1½" in from the edge of the spool.

Insert the bolt through the dowel, and thread on a nut until it's about ¹⁄₁₆" from the dowel (this allows the handle to spin freely on the bolt). Next, insert the bolt through the spool and lock it in place with the remaining nut.

PARTS LIST

Quantity	Part	Dimensions	Material
1	Bracket back	¾" × 10" × 16"	plywood
1	Bracket side	¾" × 12" × 16"	plywood
1	Bracket support	¾" × 9¼" × 11½"	plywood
2	Spool sides	¾" × 11¾"-dia. circles	plywood
8	Spool spokes	½" × 8¼"	dowels
1	Lazy Susan	7" square	metal
1	Handle sleeve	1"-dia. × 2¾"	dowel
1	Handle	⅜" × 4½"	bolt and nut

EXPLODED VIEW

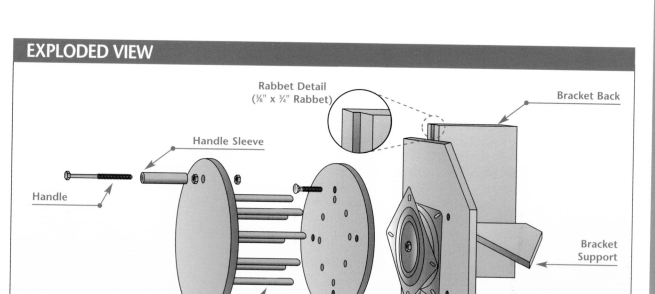

Rabbet Detail
(⅜" x ¾" Rabbet)

Handle Sleeve

Handle

Bracket Back

Bracket Support

Bracket Side

Spool Spoke

Spool Side

Lazy Susan

CHAPTER

6 MAINTENANCE

Years ago, when I was in the service, I learned the value of preventive maintenance. I spent quite a few years maintaining electronic and electromechanical communications gear, with an emphasis on the old "clunk-and-bang" teletype machines. These machines were the precursors to today's modern printers and relied heavily on moving parts; it's no wonder they required constant attention.

In our shop we had four shifts of maintenance personnel, each responsible for roughly one-fourth of the communications gear at the site. As time passed, it became readily apparent which shifts were performing their regularly scheduled maintenance, and which were not.

The gear that wasn't maintained broke down—a lot. The gear that was maintained not only had significantly fewer service calls, but also required less work when it was brought into the shop for routine maintenance.

The bottom line here is that regularly performed maintenance pays off. Your tools will run smoother, longer, and more trouble-free if you develop the habit of periodic inspection, cleaning, and lubrication.

In this chapter, I've devoted about a third of the space to maintaining the power source of your air tools, the compressor. I'll go over daily, weekly, and monthly maintenance (*see pages 85, 86, and 87, respectively*). But even with dedicated maintenance, all tools and equipment will eventually need repair. I'll cover simple repairs (like replacing a belt or repairing an air hose) and advanced work like replacing gaskets or working on the electrical system (*see pages 88–93*).

The remainder of the chapter is divided between two groups of air tools that require special attention: spray guns (*pages 94–99*) and air nailers (*pages 100–105*). Each section begins with a suggested routine for inspection, cleaning, and lubrication. This is followed by information on how to make common repairs, like replacing a bad seal.

For the more adventurous of you, I'll show you how to re-build either a spray gun or an air nailer, using a manufacturer-supplied rebuild kit.

1 Visual check One of the best compressor maintenance habits you can develop takes only a few seconds—a quick visual check of the overall condition of the compressor. What you're looking for is signs of wear that can lead to problems.

The frayed cord shown here is a good example. Not only is this a safety hazard; if let unattended, it could develop a short, causing considerable damage to the motor. Giving a compressor a once-over before you start it could prevent an expensive repair job down the road.

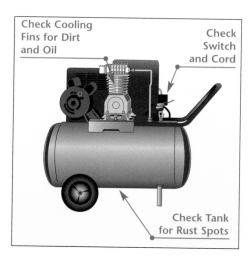

Check Cooling Fins for Dirt and Oil

Check Switch and Cord

Check Tank for Rust Spots

2 Check points There are some key points to concentrate on when performing a visual inspection of your compressor. Start with the tank or tanks. Look for chipped paint or rust that signals deterioration. If you find any, take the compressor in to a service center immediately and have it repaired.

Inspect the electrical cord carefully all the way up to the pressure switch. Check for dirt or dust clogging the cooling fins, and clean if necessary (*see page 86*). Look for oil leaking from the crankcase, and repair as necessary (*see page 88*).

3 Oil level Nothing will more seriously or quickly shorten the life of an oil-lubricated compressor than running it when it's low on oil. If you really want to extend the life of your compressor, check the oil level before each use. Here again, this takes only seconds.

Unlike a car, where it's best to check the oil when the motor is warm, you can check the oil in a compressor when it's cold. Just pull out the dipstick and note the level; refill as necessary.

Air Tools

COMPRESSOR:
WEEKLY

1 Drain the tank or tanks As we discussed earlier, when air is compressed, moisture in the air condenses to form liquid water. If you don't remove this water from the tanks, it can lead to rust and to eventual rupture.

All compressor manufacturers install petcocks or drains on the underside of the tank so that you can prevent this from happening. After you've shut your compressor down for the day, loosen the petcock to allow pressurized air in the tank to blow out any water. After a few seconds, close the petcock.

2 Check belt tension If your compressor uses an electric motor to drive the pump via a belt, it's a good idea to check the belt for proper tension on a regular basis. To do this, simply reach down and wiggle the belt to see how much it deflects.

What you're looking for here is around ½" of movement at the midway point from the belt's resting position in either direction (or 1" of movement overall). If there's more or less deflection than this, you'll need to adjust the belt; *see pages 88–89* for detailed directions.

3 Clean the compressor Although it might seem like a minor point, keeping a compressor clean does two important things. First, it makes it easy to do a visual inspection. Built-up dirt or dust can hide a developing problem. Wiping down the tank on a regular basis will prevent this. Second, when dirt and dust build up on the cooling fins of the compressor, this hinders its ability to cool itself down. Excessive heat will always shorten a machine's life. Take a moment once a week to blow out the fins with compressed air.

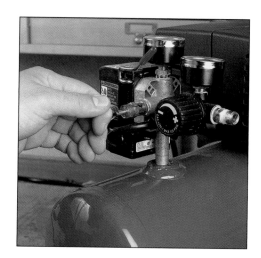

1 Check safety valve Just like the water heater in your home, every quality compressor should have a safety or pressure-relief valve that will open to drain off excessive pressure that has built up in a tank.

On a monthly basis, you should check the operation of this valve. Most valves have a pull on the valve to make this easy. With the tank filled with air, pull on the valve to make sure air can escape; if it doesn't, the valve is faulty and should replaced immediately.

2 Check flywheel and motor-pulley screws Because all compressors vibrate to a certain degree, it's a good idea to regularly check some key parts to make sure they haven't worked loose—in particular, the setscrews that hold the flywheel and motor pulley on their respective shafts.

If these were ever to vibrate loose, the belt would slip, resulting in no or reduced compressed air. Check the tension of the setscrews regularly with an Allen wrench (in most cases) or with a screwdriver.

3 Check air filter An air compressor is constantly pulling in fresh air to compress. It's the filter's job to keep the air fresh and clean. If it's clogged, one of two things will likely happen. First, the compressor's efficiency will drop because it's struggling to pull in air, just as if you'd partially covered the intake on a diver's snorkel. Second, impurities such as dirt, dust, and grease will start passing into the compressor's pump; this can cause excessive wear and even cause the pump to seize up. Check and clean the filter at least once a month.

Air Tools

COMPRESSOR REPAIRS

Since you're dealing with air under pressure, many compressor repair jobs are best left to a professional (such as rebuilding a malfunctioning pressure switch, or repairing a tank). There are, however, a number of jobs that you can take on, depending on your skill and confidence level.

I've divided these tasks into three areas: simple repairs like those shown here (replacing or adjusting a V-belt and repairing an air hose), advanced repairs (replacing a blown or leaky gasket, shown on *pages 90–91*), and electrical repairs (replacing a switch or cord, shown on *pages 92–93*).

If you don't have the time or inclination to tackle these repairs yourself, look in the yellow pages under "air compressors" to find a local repair shop. Try to locate one that's an authorized repair center for your brand of compressor. If you can't, call a shop first to make sure that they have experience working on your brand of compressor. If they do, describe your problem and see whether they have encountered the problem before and whether they can give you a rough estimate. Call around—estimates vary dramatically from shop to shop.

1 Loosen mounting bolts In order to adjust or replace the compressor's V-belt, you'll have to first loosen the mounting bolts that hold the motor in place. Depending on the manufacturer, the mounting bolts may either thread into a mounting bracket or plate (*as shown*) or else be held in place with separate nuts. In either case, loosen the bolts just enough so that you can slide the motor to adjust or remove the belt.

2 Remove and replace belt After you've slid the motor enough to loosen the belt, slip the belt off one of the pulleys and then remove it completely. If you're planning on reusing the belt, make sure to check it for signs of wear—look for cracks and missing sections. If you find any, replace the belt.

When you go to buy a new belt, make sure you buy one that's an exact replacement. Varying the length will only cause problems, since you'll be running the pump at a speed it wasn't designed to operate at.

Maintenance

3 **Adjust belt tension** After you've installed a new belt, you'll need to adjust its tension. Keeping the motor bolts friction-tight, slide the motor as far away from the pump as possible, then snug the bolts a bit tighter.

Then check the tension either by pinching the belt together at its midpoint or by pulling it gently apart. A correctly tensioned belt will deflect about ½" from a resting position.

Placing a straightedge along the belt as a reference may help in determining the amount of deflection. Once correct, fully tighten the motor mounting nuts.

AIR-HOSE REPAIR

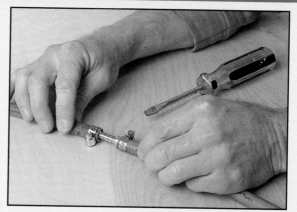

1 **Cut away damage** Since air hoses take so much abuse, it's not uncommon for one to require repair. Fortunately, there are easy-to-use repair kits available. The one shown here comes complete with barbed fittings and hose clamps.

To repair a hose, start by cutting away the damaged section with a utility knife. If you're repairing a puncture, simply cut the hose in two at the puncture. Make sure to cut cleanly through the hose, and make sure that the cut is square.

2 **Install new fitting** To install the repair fitting, first slip one hose clamp over each section of the cut hose. Then with the barbed fitting in one hand, slip the end of the fitting in the hose and push the fitting firmly until the hose bottoms out. Be assertive here—you'll have better luck if you push it all the way in at once. With the hose in place, slide each hose fitting down until it's directly over the barbed section, and then tighten the screw to lock the fitting in place.

REPLACING A BLOWN OR LEAKY GASKET

1 Drain oil A compressor that's losing compression or running rough could have a leaky or blown gasket. If you're mechanically inclined, replacing one of these isn't much harder than doing the same thing to a small internal-combustion engine, like a lawnmower. The biggest hindrance I've come across is that there's little if any documentation available (even from the manufacturer).

Fortunately, replacing gaskets isn't that difficult. To begin, remove the oil-drain plug and drain out all the oil. If necessary, tip the compressor to make sure the crankcase is empty.

2 Remove cover Where the leak or blowout is located will determine what you have to remove in order to replace the gasket. On the compressor shown here, there were two problems: The first was an oil leak at the crankcase; the other was a head gasket that didn't have good seal (*see Step 4 on the opposite page*).

To get to the leaky gasket, I had to remove the crankcase cover. To prevent a nasty oil mess, keep a rag close by to catch any stubborn oil left in the crankcase when the cover is removed.

3 Remove gasket With the cover off, gently peel the old gasket off of the crankcase. Now is a good time to inspect the crankshaft for wear and check the bottom of the crankcase to see whether there are any metal chips or impurities. Remove any you find, to prevent them from circulating with the oil.

Depending on the compressor and gasket, you may or may not need to apply gasket cement before installing the new gasket—check the owner's manual, or contact the manufacturer of the compressor.

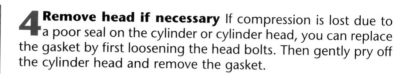

4 **Remove head if necessary** If compression is lost due to a poor seal on the cylinder or cylinder head, you can replace the gasket by first loosening the head bolts. Then gently pry off the cylinder head and remove the gasket.

Once you're here, you might as well replace the gasket beneath the valve plate. It's important to note that whenever you remove the head, you should always replace the gasket. After you've reassembled the head, use a torque wrench to tighten the head bolts (check with the compressor manufacturer for the correct torque setting).

Gaskets for compressors are available from most manufacturers, individually or in kit form. An important item to note when ordering either is that many do not come with any installation instructions. The rebuild kit that I ordered for this compressor came just as you see it here—a bag of gaskets. No instructions at all. Fortunately, most compressor manufacturers have technical support lines that you can call to get help; or if you've got Internet capabilities, you can often find help and answers for frequently asked questions on-line.

INSIDE AN AIR COMPRESSOR

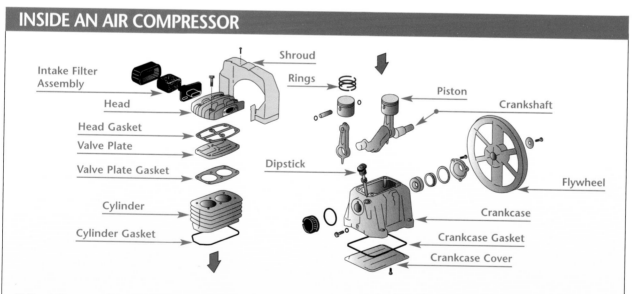

Intake Filter Assembly — Head — Head Gasket — Valve Plate — Valve Plate Gasket — Cylinder — Cylinder Gasket — Shroud — Rings — Piston — Crankshaft — Dipstick — Flywheel — Crankcase — Crankcase Gasket — Crankcase Cover

Although compressors will vary widely depending on the type and manufacturer, all have common parts. The crankcase houses the crankshaft that the flywheel is attached to, and it holds the oil that lubricates the pistons and rings as they move up in down in the cylinder. The cylinder is capped off with a valve plate and head, which are held in place with bolts. An air-intake port on the head is protected by the air filter. Gaskets maintain seals between the crankcase, its cover, the head, and the valve plate.

COMPRESSOR:
ELECTRICAL REPAIRS

1 Switch: Disconnect wiring The on/off switch on most compressors is a pressure switch. This is a pneumatically operated switch that starts and stops the motor at pre-determined pressure points. If you have a faulty switch, it's best to unplug the compressor, disconnect the switch, and have it repaired at a service center.

If you're lucky, the electrical connections are made via a snap-in connector. If not, you'll have to remove the cover (*as shown here*) to disconnect the wires. Pressure switches can be tricky. If the idea of taking one apart makes you nervous, it's best to take the compressor in to a service repair center.

2 Switch: Remove old Before you disconnect any wires from the switch, take a moment to note cable and/or wire positions, to make installing the new switch a snap. Once you've got the wires disconnected, either by removing the cable or by unscrewing the wires, you can remove the switch.

The switch will likely be attached to the compressor frame via a bracket and screws, or just screwed directly to the frame. You'll also need to loosen the compression nut on the air line running into the switch so that you can disconnect it as well.

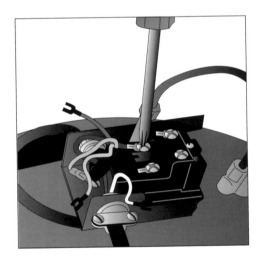

3 Switch: Install new With an identical replacement switch in hand, start by attaching it to the mounting frame or bracket. Then reconnect the air line and tighten the compression nut.

Using the notes you made earlier, hook the wires and/or cable to the appropriate terminals. Reinstall the switch cover and, with the switch in the "off" position, plug in the compressor. Now flip the compressor on and check to make sure that it cycles properly.

1 **Electrical cord: Remove old plug** If you find that the electrical cord for your compressor needs repair, there are two options: replace the plug, or replace the entire cord. Which option you choose will depend on where the damage is and how long the cord is.

If the damage is near the plug and you've got plenty of cord, you can snip off the cord at the damaged area and install a new plug (*see Step 2 below*). If the damage requires a new cord, see Step 3 *below.*

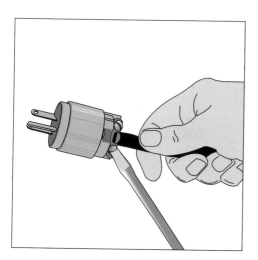

2 **Electrical cord: Install new plug** After you've cut off the damaged section of cord, trim about 1½" of insulation off the cut end. Then slip the cover of the new plug over the cord, and strip ½" of insulation off each wire.

Insert the wires in their respective slots (black to brass, white to silver, and green to green), or wrap the wires around screw terminals and tighten the screws. Slide the two halves of the plug together, and tighten the mounting screws. If strain relief is separate, tighten the screws of the clamp.

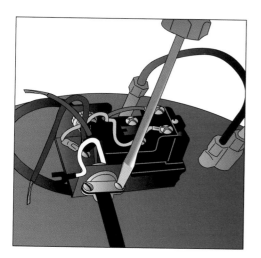

3 **Electrical cord: Replace cord instead** If it's necessary to replace the entire electrical cord, unplug it and remove the cover for the pressure switch. Unscrew each of the screw terminals, making sure to note which wire goes where.

Then connect the new cord to the appropriate terminals, tighten the screws, and replace the cover. Another option is to replace one of the old wires at a time with wires from the new cord. Plug the compressor in and test for proper operation

Air Tools

SPRAY GUNS:
CLEANING

1 Unscrew canister It's extremely important that you clean a spray gun immediately after using it, since the material in it can dry quickly, particularly in the small passages inside the gun.

If you don't clean it right away, the material can set up and render the spray gun useless. Believe me, it's very difficult to remove material that has hardened from the small passages within the gun.

The first step to cleaning a spray gun is to turn off the air compressor. If you're using the gun in the siphon mode (*as shown*), unscrew the canister and lift off the gun.

Depress the trigger, and wait a few moments for the material in the supply tube to drain back into the canister. Then drain any remaining canister contents back into the original can.

To clean a pressure feed gun with a remote cup or tank, first turn off the air to the cup or tank. Then release material pressure from the system by opening the relief valve.

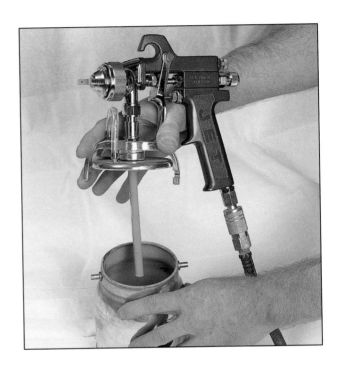

2 Rinse out canister Now you can rinse the canister out with the appropriate solvent; lacquer thinner for lacquer; mineral spirits for oil-based paints; and warm, soapy water for latex paints and water-based finishes.

If there's any doubt about what type of solvent to use, check the label on the can. Note: Not all thinners can be used as solvents—here again, check the label. Rinse the canister thoroughly, and finish with a rinse of fresh solvent.

If you're using a remote cup or tank, you'll also need to clean out the hoses. You can manually backflush the hoses into the cup or tank with solvent by following the manufacturer's directions in the owner's manual.

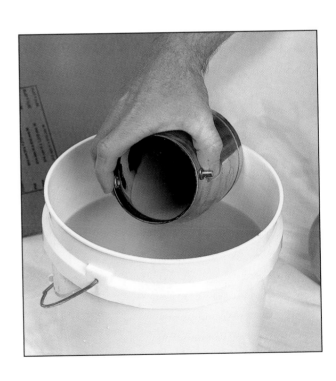

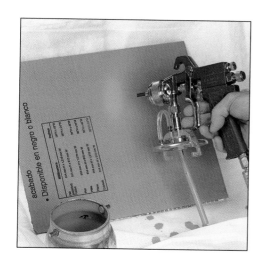

3 Pull trigger and drain The next step is to set up a cleaning area where you can spray old paint and solvent. A drop cloth draped over a cardboard box works well. Make to sure the work surface you're using won't be harmed by paint or solvent soaking through a drop cloth—add a plastic liner under the cloth, or set everything up on a scrap piece of plywood on sawhorses.

Holding the spray gun over the drop cloth, pull the trigger to release any remaining fluid. Continue spraying until no more material comes out of the gun.

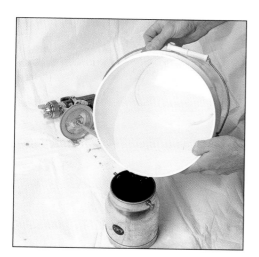

4 Refill canister with clean solvent After the remaining material has been sprayed out of the gun, fill the canister about half full with the appropriate solvent.

Remote cups and tanks should be cleaned as well, using the same procedure described here. In either case, take the time to wipe off the exterior of the cup or tank with a clean rag dipped in solvent.

5 Spray until clear Attach the canister to the gun, and spray until the solvent runs clear. Shake the gun vigorously up and down and from side to side as you spray.

Once the spray begins to clear, shoot the solvent back into a pail or bucket and discard the used solvent according to your local regulations. When the canister is empty, repeat Steps 4 and 5 with fresh solvent. Depending on what you've been spraying, you may need to do this three or four times.

6 Wipe the body clean When the solvent finally runs clear and the canister is empty, disconnect the air line and remove the canister. Dip a clean cloth in fresh solvent, and wipe down the exterior of the can and the body of the gun.

Pay particular attention to the seal inside the rim of the lid. The condition of this rubber seal can make the difference between an easy spray job and a difficult one. Use a toothbrush dipped in solvent to remove any stubborn residue. Then dry the parts and set them aside.

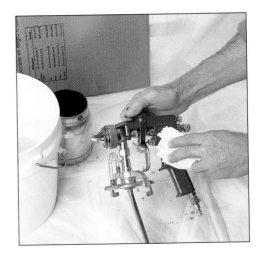

7 Remove the air cap seal and clean Finally, remove the air cap retaining nut (if your gun has one) and the air cap. Thoroughly clean the threads on the body that the air cap attaches to, and clean the air cap (*see the sidebar below*).

Never use a sharp metal object to clean the air cap—doing so will damage it, resulting in improper spray patterns. When everything is clean and dry, reassemble the gun and store it in a clean, dry place.

CLEANING AIR CAPS

There are two common ways to safely clean an air cap that's accumulated a buildup of finish. One method is to soak the air cap in the appropriate thinner, overnight if possible. This will usually loosen any stubborn particles. Second, you can dip the air cap in solvent and, with a toothbrush and a little elbow grease, scrub the stubborn finish off. Or, combine the two: Soak the cap for an hour or two and then scrub.

Although most folks realize the importance of cleaning a spray gun properly, many don't know that lubrication is just as important. The solvents you use to clean a spray gun will often remove lubrication along with the paint or finish. Because of this, it's important to re-lubricate the necessary parts. This is particularly necessary if you've had to disassemble the gun in order to clean it properly.

Not only is lubrication important to keep moving parts running smoothly, it also can serve to make disassembly or assembly easier (such as adding a drop of oil to the threads of an air cap; *see below*). A thin coat of oil will also help protect metal surfaces from rust, especially if you've been spraying water-based finishes.

Virtually any light machine oil will do the job; but if you prefer, you can purchase air-tool oil or special oil that's just for use with spray guns. Remember that oil can and will dry out over time. So if you haven't used your sprayer for a while, make sure to lubricate it first before you begin to spray.

1 Moving parts or threads Any part of your spray gun that has threads or moves should be lubricated after every cleaning. Use a silicone-free lubricant to avoid a common finishing problem called "fish-eye." Apply a few drops of oil to the threads of the air cap nut as you reassemble the gun.

Apply a drop or two to moving parts like the air-adjustment knob, the fluid-adjustment knob, the trigger-bearing screw, the air-valve rod and trigger, and the air-valve and fluid-needle packing (*see the drawing on page 26*).

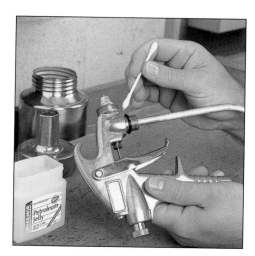

2 O-rings If you've disassembled the gun for cleaning, it's important to replenish the lubricant on the O-rings that you removed during cleaning. (Lacquer thinner in particular will virtually suck the lubricant and moisture out of a rubber O-ring.)

You can buy a special O-ring lubricant where you purchased your sprayer, or do what I do: Use ordinary petroleum jelly. Wipe a generous coat on the O-ring with a Q-Tip or with your finger, and roll the O-ring in place.

Air Tools

SPRAY GUNS:
REBUILDING

1 Replace O-rings To rebuild or repair a spray gun, start by removing the canister and the lid from the gun (if possible). Have the exploded view from your owner's manual in front of you as you work; take it slow so that reassembling the gun will be easier.

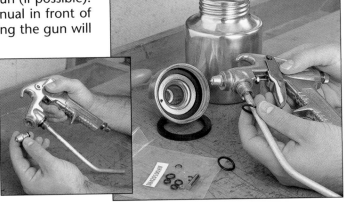

If you're using a rebuild kit (*see the sidebar on page 99*), you'll likely be replacing all the O-rings. The O-ring shown here creates the seal between the fluid inlet and the lid of the cup. The O-ring in the inset is the seal between the fluid tip and the gun.

2 Remove adjusting knob The next step is to remove the fluid-adjusting knob (*see the drawing on page 26* to identify common spray-gun parts). Slowly turn the knob counterclockwise to loosen it. As you near the end of the threads, keep a firm grip on both the knob and the gun because the knob applies pressure to the fluid needle spring, which will force the knob out quickly once it's loose. Set the knob aside.

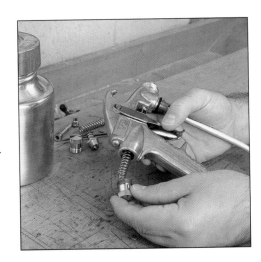

Shop Tip: An empty egg carton makes a great container for small parts.

3 Pull out the fluid needle Once the knob has been removed, pull out the fluid-needle spring. Then carefully grab the exposed end of the fluid needle and pull it gently out. Be extremely careful with the fluid needle if you're planning on reusing it: It's precisely machined, and if you drop it on a hard surface, it'll get damaged. If this does happen, replace it. If you're rebuilding the gun, the kit will likely include a new fluid tip. (I recommend saving the old one if it's in good shape, for an emergency repair.)

4 **Replace sleeve** Most rebuild kits come with a replacement fluid-needle sleeve. This is the part which houses the fluid needle so that it can slide in and out smoothly. It's often made of brass.

On many spray guns, the sleeve is held in place with a spring clip or a nut. Once this has been removed, you can push the sleeve out of the gun. Here again, if the part doesn't show excessive wear, hang on to it for future repair work.

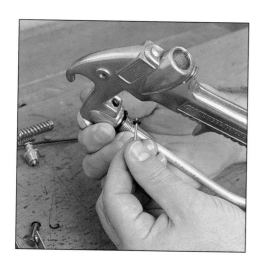

5 **Replace packing** One of the smallest parts in a rebuild kit is one of the most important: the fluid needle packing. It's often a tiny leather washer. The fluid needle runs through this washer on its way to the air cap. When a lubricant is applied to the packing, it swells, forming a tight seal. Whenever you replace the fluid needle, you should replace the packing.

Now you can begin reassembling the spray gun. Take your time and consult the exploded view as required—and don't forget to lubricate as you go.

SPRAY-GUN REBUILD KITS

Depending on the compressor manufacturer, a rebuild kit for a spray gun may come with explicit instructions, or, like the one shown here, with nothing but parts in a bag.

With this in mind, it's always a good idea when ordering a rebuild kit like this to make sure it includes directions. If it doesn't, find out who you need to speak to in customer support or technical support to get a detailed set of instructions.

FASTENING TOOLS:
CLEANING

Just as with compressors and spray guns, keeping an air nailer clean is an important maintenance task that will pay off in the long run. Not only will an air nailer that's clean be more dependable, it'll save you time because there'll be less of a tendency toward nail jams.

Nail jams are often caused by dirt and debris in and around the nosepiece and drive-pin areas. Keeping these areas clean and well lubricated (*see page 102*) will have a huge impact on the performance of the nailer. Here again, follow a set maintenance routine that if done often enough will develop into a habit.

The entire routine described here will take less than a minute to complete—not much to invest to keep up an expensive tool. The other thing that cleaning and lubrication promotes is visual inspection. Giving your nailer a quick once-over every time you clean it will help catch small problems before they develop into expensive repairs. Keep an eye out for wear that can signal the beginning of a problem.

1 Clean the magazine When you're done using an air nailer, disconnect the air line and open up the magazine. Remove any fasteners, and then attach a blow gun to the air line and give the magazine a couple of blasts of air to clear out any dust and debris.

Just as you should never store a handgun loaded with bullets, you can prevent accidents by not storing a nail gun that's loaded with fasteners. Keep the magazine empty; this will also remind you to blow it out again before you load in the new fasteners.

2 Clean the nosepiece The nosepiece of an air nailer is particularly susceptible to dirt and debris. A few blasts with a blow gun will prevent a lot of problems. Not only should you do this at the end of a day, you should also do this periodically when you're using the gun heavily.

I like to keep a blow gun in my tool belt so that every time I load fasteners, I can blow out both the magazine and the nosepiece. This might sound like overkill, but I've been using the same nailer for years now—maintenance like this does pay off.

3 Plug the intake In the typical air nailer, air flows in through the intake and up into the cylinder, forcing a piston and pin to drive a nail. Any impurities that tag along in the air will be injected into the cylinder.

The cylinder, piston, and driver pin are all precision-machined parts that operate on tight tolerances. Think of the havoc a chuck of sawdust or other debris could cause if it got inside. To prevent this from happening, always plug the intake of your nailer as soon as you're done using it.

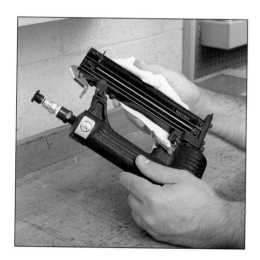

4 Wipe off the body With the intake plugged and the inside of the nailer clean, take a couple seconds to wipe off the exterior of the gun with a clean, soft cloth. (I keep one in the nail gun case just for this purpose.)

Again, this is a good time to check the nailer visually for signs of excessive wear. Look for shiny spots, which are the telltale indicators that something is wrong. If you suspect a problem, consult your owner's manual or a local tool repair shop.

5 Store the nailer properly Finally, always store your air nailer in a sturdy case to keep it clean and protect it from damage. If your nailer didn't come with a case, there are a number of after-market cases and totes available—you can often find these where you bought your nailer or in mail-order tool catalogs.

If you prefer, you can make your own case. For detailed instructions on how to build a shop-made case for your nailer, see *pages 80–81*.

FASTENING TOOLS:
LUBRICATING

Most air nailers require both internal and external lubrication to run smoothly. Internal lubrication can accomplished by three methods: a lubricator that's built into the system, a small in-line oiler that's attached directly to the fastening tool, or injecting oil to the intake of the tool before use. (Note: Adding oil to the intake is generally seen as a supplement to one of the automatic lubricators mentioned above, not as a replacement.)

Before using any of these methods of internal lubrication, check your owner's manual to make sure that your nailer requires it. Some manufacturers have introduced "oil-free" or "permanently oiled" nailers that require no internal lubrication. Injecting oil into these nailers can actually cause damage.

Regardless of whether your nailer requires internal lubrication or not, all fastening tools will work better and last longer if the external moving parts and linkages receive periodic lubrication. Here again, check the owner's manual to see what the manufacturer recommends.

1 Feed oil in line If you don't have a lubricator built into your air system (*see page 22*) that automatically injects oil into the air line, the next closest thing is an in-line oiler like the one shown here. In-line oilers attach directly to a gun and accept a standard air hose.

Since they hold much less oil than a full-sized lubricator, you have to keep an eye on the oil level. In-line oilers are particularly useful for larger guns like a framing or coil nailer, which drives big fasteners.

2 Inject oil in air intake Another option to keep the interior parts of an air nailer running smoothly is simply to inject some oil into the nailer manually. How much and how often you inject oil depends on the gun and the type of work you're doing.

If you're using a brad nailer to fasten parts together, a couple of drops at the beginning of the job will do. If you're using a coil nailer to install roofing shingles, it's best to add oil every time you refill the magazine.

3 Apply oil Before you apply any lubricant, check your owner's manual to see what the manufacturer recommends (typically it's S.A.E. no. 20-weight). Virtually all manufacturers will warn you to steer clear of detergent oils. Regular air tool oil will do, but it's often very light and won't last long.

I like to apply oil or a thin coating of lightweight grease to the lubrication points and then wipe off any excess with a clean rag right before I put a nailer back in its case. If it has been in storage for a while, I'll lubricate it before using it again.

LUBRICATION POINTS

In addition to the internal parts of the nailer that need lubrication to run well, there are numerous external linkages and moving parts that will benefit from periodic attention.

In particular, the magazine mechanism, the nosepiece area and associated safety linkages, and the trigger area need to be lubricated from time to time. Consult your owner's manual for the recommended lubricant and lubrication points and to see how often it should be applied.

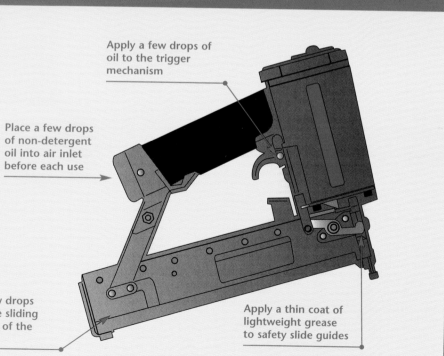

Apply a few drops of oil to the trigger mechanism

Place a few drops of non-detergent oil into air inlet before each use

Apply a few drops of oil to the sliding mechanism of the magazine

Apply a thin coat of lightweight grease to safety slide guides

FASTENING TOOLS:
REPLACING O-RINGS

1 Disassemble With heavy use, the internal seals in an air nailer will wear out, and you'll begin to lose compression. The nailer won't run as smoothly, and even with adequate air pressure, it won't fully drive nails.

When this happens, it's time to replace the internal O-rings. Many manufacturers offer these in kit form (hopefully, with instructions). With the air disconnected from the nailer, use an Allen wrench or a screwdriver to remove the screws that hold down the cap that covers the cylinder.

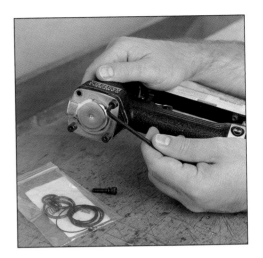

2 Replace O-rings Gently pull off the cap. There's usually an O-ring on the underside of the cap, which maintains the seal on the cylinder (*as shown*). If you've purchased a rebuild kit, replace each O-ring in turn as you continue to disassemble the gun. Keep the old and new O-rings separate to prevent mixing them up.

As you replace each O-ring, apply a generous amount of O-ring grease or ordinary petroleum jelly to each O-ring. When done, reverse the steps you took to disassemble the nailer to put it back together.

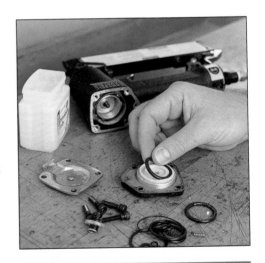

INSIDE AN AIR NAILER

Air flows into a nailer via the intake port. From there, it travels up into a chamber. When both the safety mechanism and the trigger are depressed, the air vents out of the chamber and forces the cylinder and attached driver blade down.

As the driver blade moves downward, it strikes the next fastener in line, forcing it into the workpiece. At the completion of the driving action, incoming air forces the cylinder and the driver blade to return to their starting position to await the next cycle.

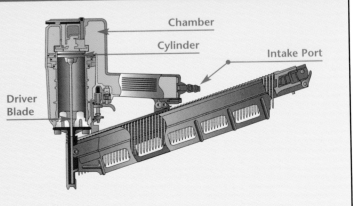

Chamber
Cylinder
Intake Port
Driver Blade

Maintenance

Since the driver blade in a nailer is constantly striking fasteners, it will eventually wear out over time. Fortunately, replacing a driver blade is a fairly simple task.

Many nail gun manufacturers offer replacement driver blades in a kit with various O-rings. Some of the makers of large nailers don't sell replacement parts at all—you'll either have to take your nailer to an authorized service center for repair or try and get parts from them.

Although most nailers are fairly straightforward in design, it's best to take your time whenever you work on one. It's also a good idea to have the exploded view of the nailer from the owner's manual in front of you while you work.

Whenever possible, thread screws you've removed back into the holes they came from as soon as you've removed the part. This is a surefire way to save time trying to figure out which screw goes where.

1 Remove cover To replace a driver blade, start by removing the screws that hold the cap in place on the top of the cylinder. If the screws that hold the cap on your nailer are slotted or Phillips-head, remove them with the appropriate screwdriver and then replace the screws with Allen screws purchased from your local hardware store.

Since fasteneing tools are subjected to a lot of percussion, the screws can really lock down tight over time. An Allen screw provides a better purchase for tightening or loosening, with less risk of stripping.

2 Replace driver blade Once the cap is removed, reach into the cylinder and gently pull out the driver blade. Before installing the replacement, apply a coat of petroleum jelly or O-ring lubricant to the O-ring.

With the driver blade in the cylinder, apply a lubricant to the O-ring seal on the cap and place it on the cylinder. Add the cap screws and tighten them. Without fasteners in the nailer, hook up the air line and test operation. If all is well, disconnect the air line and load fasteners in the magazine. Hook the air back up and test it.

SOLVING COMMON PROBLEMS

When I first got into wood-working and general home improvement work years ago, I always blamed myself if something didn't go just right. Whether it was a cut that wasn't straight, a part that ended up slightly askew, or a door or a drawer that didn't open or close the way I wanted it to, it was my fault.

A decade of experience later, the pendulum had swung the other way: It was the tool's fault. Yeah, that's it, it was the tool, all right. Well, sometimes it was; but now, over two decades from when I started, I realize that common problems most often are caused by a combination of the two: the tool and the technique. And a lot of time, it's something small. The old "hey, if you hold the tool like this…it won't do that anymore." Or "you know, if you flip that little lever, it'll stop buzzing."

It's a shame that many of the tool manufacturers don't provide better troubleshooting information in their manuals. I guess they all figure we instinctively know how to use their tools—and that nothing will ever go wrong. Yeah, right.

In this chapter, I'll provide you with that missing information. I'll start by describing the most common problems you'll have with your compressor, and their solutions. Everything from knocking and excessive vibration to dealing with a compressor that cycles too often (*pages 107–113*).

Then, on to probably the most complicated to use air-powered tool, the spray gun. I'll cover how to correct bad spray patterns, what to do about pinholes and blushing and finish with overspray, and preventing the all-too-common sags and runs (*see pages 114–121*).

Finally, I'll delve into the everyday problems that you're likely to encounter when using an air nailer—annoying problems like crooked fasteners, splitting wood, shooting multiple fasteners, and nailers whose nosepiece dents the workpiece (*see pages 122, 123, 124, and 125, respectively*).

1 Needs oil A compressor that knocks or pings may simply be telling you it needs oil. Of course, this shouldn't happen if you're checking the oil on a daily basis. But if it does, check the oil level and top it off with the appropriate grade oil (check your owner's manual for recommended type).

If the oil level checked fine recently but it's down significantly, inspect the compressor for signs of a blown seal or oil leaks, and take corrective action as needed (*see pages 90–91*).

2 Loose pulley The pulleys on most compressors attach to the motor by way of a setscrew that locks a key into a channel or groove in both the pulley and the motor shaft.

With use, the setscrew can loosen and the key can vibrate loose and cause knocking. If you work your compressor hard, you should check the motor and pulley setscrews on a monthly basis.

3 Loose flywheel Just like the motor pulley, the flywheel that attaches to the compressor pump can work its way loose over time. In most cases, the flywheel is held in place with a bolt; tightening this with a socket wrench will take care of the knocking problem.

The most common cause for a flywheel loosening in the first place is a pulley and flywheel that are out of alignment. Make sure to check this whenever you adjust belt tension; *see page 109* for more on this.

Air Tools

COMPRESSOR:
EXCESSIVE VIBRATION

All air compressors vibrate to some extent. But a compressor that won't stay put, or that shakes like a washing machine with an unbalanced load, is too much. A compressor that vibrates excessively is like a child that cries when sick: It needs attention.

Excessive vibration is a sure sign that something is wrong and that it's going to get worse if you don't attend to it immediately. Fortunately, it's relatively easy to identify and fix many of the common causes of air compressor vibration.

Performing routine preventive maintenance on your compressor will catch many of the problems described here before they even get a chance to develop into trouble (*see pages 85–87 for more on this*).

1 Mounting bolts are loose A running motor exerts a lot of strain on the bolts that secure it to its frame. Over time, it's not uncommon for these mounting bolts to work loose. This is one of the first things to check if your compressor is starting to vibrate excessively.

If you find that they've worked loose, consider adding lock washers to the bolts before you tighten them. If these don't prevent the bolts from working loose again, it'll at least take the bolts longer to work loose.

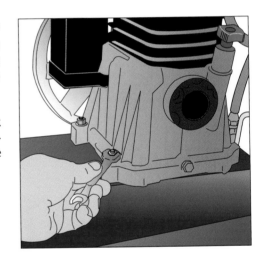

2 Compressor isn't level I've got a little oil-less compressor that, if it's not perfectly level, will skitter across the floor like a kid's toy. Most compressors have rubber feet or pads that can adjust somewhat to an uneven floor. But they can only compensate so much.

To check to make sure your compressor is level, push down on the corners alternately to see if it rocks. If it does, first try moving it around a bit to find a level spot. If this doesn't work, slip a carpenter's shim under the pad, foot, or wheel at the low spot.

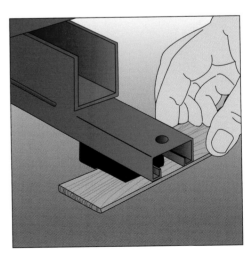

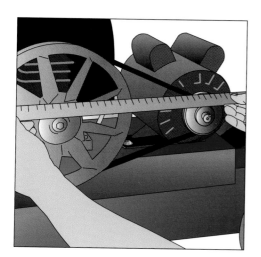

3 **Pulley and flywheel are misaligned** Another common cause of motor vibration is a motor pulley and compressor flywheel that aren't aligned. To check for this, hold a straight-edge across the outer edges of the flywheel, as shown, so that it extends toward the motor pulley.

Measure the gap between the straightedge and the belt near the flywheel and the pulley. If they're not the same, loosen the motor-mounting bolts and adjust the position of the motor so the gap is even. Then tighten the bolts.

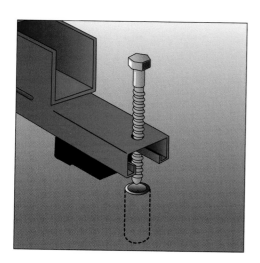

4 **Secure the compressor** A simple way to help reduce a compressor's vibration is to secure it to the floor; although this doesn't eliminate vibration, it does reduce it by transferring it to the building's foundation.

On a cement floor like the one shown, this means first drilling holes in the floor with a masonry bit to accept lag shields. Then slip in the lag shields, thread a bolt through each mounting hole, and tighten.

For wood floors, a lag bolt will get the job done. Be careful not to overtighten the bolts so that you don't crush the rubber pads or feet.

5 **Bent shaft** If you've checked all of the other possibilities shown here and your compressor still vibrates, it could be caused by a bent motor shaft or crankshaft.

You can check the motor by clamping a block of wood up against the shaft as shown. Then slip a feeler gauge between the shaft and the block, and slowly rotate the motor shaft. A noticeable gap means that the shaft is bent and needs to be replaced; this is best done at a repair shop. This same method can be used to check the crankshaft.

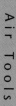

COMPRESSOR:
OVERHEATS

1 Check the thermal reset Whenever you work a compressor too hard, it heats up. When it gets to the point where the heat can damage the motor, a built-in thermal reset will pop. This is basically a bimetal strip that opens when a certain temperature is reached.

If this happens, you'll have to let the compressor cool down before you can reset the switch. If the thermal reset pops repeatedly, you'll have to either work slower, take more breaks, or use a tool that demands less cfm.

2 Compressor is low on oil Another reason for a compressor to overheat is that it's low on oil. Here again, this should not happen if you're checking the oil on a daily basis. If you catch the heat buildup quick enough, just top off the oil and let the compressor cool down.

If lack of oil was the problem, and the compressor heated up to the point where the thermal reset popped, chances are high that internal damage occurred. In this case, I'd suggest you take the compressor in to a local service repair center to be looked at by a technician.

3 Valve may be sticking There are a number of valves in a compressor that, if they malfunction, can cause heat to build up. In particular, when exhaust valves stick or seize up, they don't allow the compressed air to flow out to the tank. This can quickly cause heat to build up, and it requires immediate attention. If parts are available and you're mechanically inclined, you can replace them yourself (*see pages 90–91*). Otherwise, take the compressor to a service center.

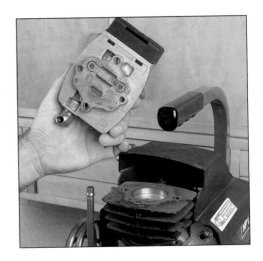

4 **Air filter is clogged** When an air filter is clogged, the compressor is struggling to breathe. The pump has to work a lot harder to draw in sufficient air to compress. The result of this extra effort is strained parts and a rapid buildup of heat.

The solution is to remove and clean the air filter. If you're working in a particularly dusty or dirty setting, like a woodworking shop or a job site where drywall is being sanded, check and clean the air filter daily.

5 **Add a lighter-viscosity oil** If the oil that you fill the crankcase up with is too heavy, the internal parts will move slower and work harder—sort of like trying to run in a swimming pool.

Check in the owner's manual for your compressor to see what the manufacturer recommends. Drain the oil according to the manufacturer's directions, and refill the crankcase with the correct weight and grade.

6 **Not enough air circulation** An air compressor (like the one shown) that's been shoehorned into a tight space and then covered with junk is like wrapping a coat around a motorcycle engine that's air-cooled and then taking it out for a ride.

In both cases, the engine or pump needs air to flow past its cooling fins to pull heat away. When no air can flow past the compressor, heat won't be able to dissipate, and it will soon overheat. *See page 45* for recommendations on locating and setting up a compressor.

COMPRESSOR: TANK DOESN'T HOLD PRESSURE

Probably the most frequent reason why the tank on an air compressor won't maintain pressure is that there's a leak in the air line. If you suspect that this is the problem, first eliminate as much of the line as possible by closing valves or removing air hose.

If you've got an end cap on hand, thread it onto the air outlet of the compressor to close off the air completely. Then turn on the compressor and watch the pressure gauge. If it goes down, you've got a leak somewhere; *see the steps below.*

Once you've eliminated both the check valve and the fittings, and the tank still won't hold pressure, you may have a blown seal or gasket in the compressor pump, or the tank itself may have a pinhole in it. If the problem is a blown seal, you may want to fix it yourself (*see pages 90–91*) or take it in for service. If the tank is the problem, stop using the compressor immediately and take it in to a nearby service repair center.

1 **Check the pressure-relief valve** Unfortunately, when a pressure-relief valve goes bad, it usually does it gradually. The constant pressure beating on the valve will eventually win the war, and the valve will slowly begin to leak air past its seal.

If you think this may be why your tank isn't holding pressure, apply some soapy water to the valve—bubbles indicate a leak. If the valve is faulty, replace it immediately or have it replaced at a service center.

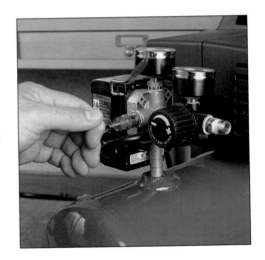

2 **Check the compression fittings** More common than a faulty relief valve, loose fittings will often allow air to leak out of your system and not allow the tank to maintain a steady pressure. The constant vibration of the compressor will eventually cause this to happen.

Whenever I do a monthly checkup on my large compressor, I like to snug up all the compression fittings with an adjustable wrench. It takes only a few seconds, and it can prevent leakage problems down the road.

COMPRESSOR:
CYCLES TOO OFTEN

A compressor that cycles too often is the most common complaint I hear. Let's face it, compressors are loud. And one that seems to run all the time is even worse. Most compressors are rated for a 50-percent duty cycle; that is, on for half the time and off the other half. If your compressor is running more than 50 percent of the time, you're going to decrease its life span considerably.

I describe *below* the two most common reasons a compressor runs too often. If neither of these is the cause, the problem may be that the compressor is running too fast. About the only way this can happen is if a belt or a pulley on the compressor was replaced recently with an improper part. Consult your owner's manual or the compressor manufacturer if you think this may be the problem.

1 Water in tank Let's say you've got a compressor with twin tanks. If you removed one of the tanks, would the compressor have to run more often? Sure, less storage space means the tank empties faster when used, and the compressor has to kick on more often.

Although this is an extreme example, the same thing will happen if you allow condensed moisture to build up in your tanks. The water will take up the air's storage space. Draining the tank daily will prevent this.

2 Not enough compressor The number one reason a compressor cycles too often is that you don't have enough compressor for the job. A good example is the setup shown here. This little oil-less compressor puts out 2.3 cfm at 90 psi. The random-orbit sander hooked up to it needs 7 cfm.

In a situation like this, the compressor will run virtually nonstop trying to keep up with the sander. This is bad for both the sander and the compressor. It's time for either a larger compressor or hand-sanding.

SPRAY GUN:
PATTERN TOP-HEAVY

1 Horn is plugged When you experience spray patterns that are top-heavy when using an external-mix cap, it's often due to plugged holes in the horn of the air cap.

There are a few things that can cause this. First, trying to spray too thick of a material (thin it according to the instructions on the label). Second, debris in the material to be sprayed (proper straining should take care of this; *see page 62*). And third, the finish you're spraying may be too fast-drying (*see page 117*).

2 Fluid tip is damaged Another reason a spray gun will produce a top-heavy pattern is that the fluid tip may be damaged or that it may not be matched to the air cap. To check for damage, disconnect the air line, release the pressure from the canister, and remove the air cap.

If necessary, remove the fluid-control knob and pull out the fluid tip (*see pages 98–99*). Otherwise, check your owner's manual or contact the manufacturer to find out whether the fluid tip is matched to the air cap.

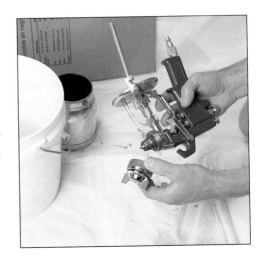

3 Air-cap seal Occasionally, the seal between the air cap and the spray gun can cause an odd pattern. If you suspect this, it's best to remove the air-cap retainer and the air cap (with the air hose disconnected and canister pressure released) and clean them.

When dry, add a drop or two of light oil to the threads of the spray gun, and screw the air-cap retainer and air cap back in place.

1 Problem When a spray gun creates a pattern that is heavy to the left or the right, the problem is caused by either a dirty air cap or a clogged orifice.

To determine which is the problem, rotate the air cap 180° and spray again. If the pattern remains the same, the problem is caused by material buildup at the fluid tip (*see Step 3 below*). If the pattern changes with air-cap movement, the air cap is the culprit and needs to be cleaned.

2 Air cap is dirty The most thorough way to clean an air cap is to soak it in solvent overnight. However, when time is a factor, you can try scrubbing the air cap clean with a toothbrush dipped in solvent.

If possible, let the air cap soak for at least five minutes to help loosen the obstruction. Make sure you wear eye protection when you do this, as the bristles of a toothbrush can splatter solvent in every direction.

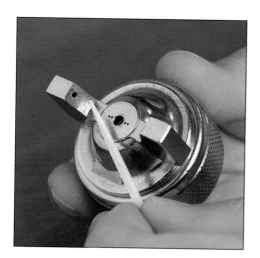

3 Orifice is clogged An obstruction at the fluid tip can occur either around the tip or inside the air cap. Either way, you'll need to first remove the air cap.

The best tool I've found for clearing an obstruction is an ordinary round toothpick. Its sharp point allows me to get into even the smallest air-cap orifice, yet it can't scratch or damage any of the metal parts.

Air Tools

SPRAY GUN:
PINHOLES

Small holes in the surface of a dried finish, or "pinholes," are most often found after a solvent-based finish has been applied. In many cases, it's the either because of holding the gun too close to the surface (*see below*) or because the finish wasn't thinned properly (*see the sidebar below*).

Another reason that pinholes occur is that the surface wasn't prepped properly. This is especially prevalent in open-grained woods like the wood at left in the photo. The solution here is to apply pore filler or spray sealer to the surface before spraying.

Gun is too close As a general rule of thumb, you should hold a spray gun 8" to 12" away from the surface you're spraying. If a ruler isn't handy, use your hand as shown. The typical distance from outstretched thumb to the end of your middle finger will get you in the ballpark.

Remember to hold the spray gun parallel to the surface as you move it from side to side. Tilting the sprayer up or down can also create a heavy coat that can also result in pinholes.

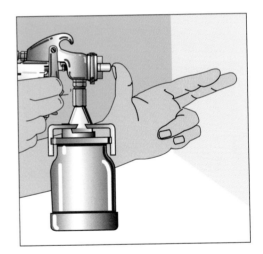

THINNING FINISHES

Although most finish manufacturers list the correct thinning agent right on the can, some don't. If this is the case and you can't find out easily what thinner to use, the general guideline is to thin the finish with the same material you would use to clean it up with.

For example, if the can says to use mineral spirits to clean up brushes, you can most likely use it to thin the finish. I'd recommend trying this first on a small sample before adding it to the entire can. Note: Most water-based finishes suggest that you thin them with special thinners or additives. In a pinch, a small amount of water will do.

1 **Finish is too fast-drying** Blushing of a finish—a milky white clouded area—is the result of moisture being trapped under a fast-drying finish. You'll most often experience this when spraying lacquer, since it dries so fast.

In many cases, blushing occurs when lacquer is sprayed on a hot, humid day. As the lacquer hits the hot surface, the solvent evaporates and quickly cools the surface. This rapid cooling causes water droplets to form on the surface. It's these water droplets that get trapped under the finish as you continue to spray.

2 **Retarder** If you suspect that the humidity is too high to safely spray lacquer, consider spraying on a less humid day. If this isn't possible, you can add lacquer retarder to the finish.

Lacquer retarder is a slow-drying thinner that, when mixed with lacquer, slows down the drying time of the finish sufficiently to allow moisture to escape from the surface. Follow the directions on the retarder to mix in the appropriate amount.

3 **Blush eraser** If you don't notice a blushing problem until after the fact, you can still try to release the moisture trapped in the finish. Some lacquer manufacturers sell a blush "eraser" in a spray can.

When the eraser is sprayed on the blush area, it redissolves the finish and should allow the moisture to work its way out. Another option if you don't have any blush eraser on hand is to spray on a light coat of full-strength lacquer retarder. This will also redissolve the finish to allow mositure out.

Air Tools

SPRAY GUN:
OVERSPRAY

No matter how careful you are, the very nature of spraying a finish will create some overspray. As I mentioned in Chapter 4, a certain amount of overspray is necessary with proper technique. You need to release the trigger about 6" past the edge of the surface. If you're doing this, and you notice that you've experienced spray significantly past where you've released the trigger, you've got a problem; *see below.*

Something else worth mentioning here is that you need to protect your clothes from picking up and transferring this overspray around your shop or home. I have a sort of "uniform" that I use just for spraying: an old pair of sneakers, plus a flannel shirt and pair of jeans that should have been thrown away years ago but are still comfortable. Take care to change out of these before entering the house.

1 Atomizing pressure is too high Overspray is often caused by using too high an atomizing pressure. Many manufacturers of finish (especially those who know their finish is likely to be sprayed) will often make a note on the label of the can indicating the recommended pressure for spraying.

If this isn't the case, try decreasing the compressor pressure a few pounds. You'll most likely need to readjust fluid and air control to get proper material flowing.

2 Fluid pressure is too low Another reason overspray occurs is that the pressure of the fluid coming into the gun is too low when you're using the gun in pressure-feed mode. There are a couple reason for this. First, the pressure to the material tank or pot may simply need to be increased slightly. Second, the tube that carries fluid from the material tank to the gun may be too long or be clogged.

Check the owner's manual of the material tank for recommended maximum length of hose. If it's okay, the material tube may be clogged; remove it and flush it out.

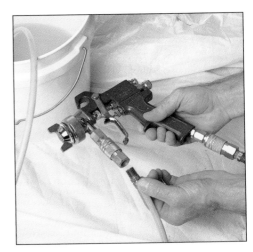

3 **Spraying past the work surface** Although it may seem obvious, many instances of overspray result from spraying too far past the edge of the surface. Proper technique calls for a bit of overspray: typically 6" to 8".

If you're experiencing more than that, it may be that all you have to do is work on releasing the trigger soon after the gun passes the edge.

4 **Wrong air cap** Just like many other spraying problems, a wrong air cap–fluid tip combination can cause overspray. Here again, check with the manufacturer of the spray gun to determine which air cap should be used with which fluid tip. Correct as needed.

5 **Check the viscosity of the material** Material that's too thick or too thin can't atomize properly and can result in overspray. Use a viscosity cup to check the material you're spraying, to see whether it's correct (*see page 62* for more on viscosity). Replace the fluid with thicker material or add thinner as necessary.

SPRAY GUN:
SAGS OR RUNS

1 Problem Who hasn't had the unpleasant experience of watching in horror as a freshly spray-painted surface begins to sag or run? I know I have, particularly when using a can of spray paint.

One of the many advantages a spray gun offers over a can is that you're much more in control of how the paint gets applied, especially in terms of fluid and air pressure. That's not to say that technique can't be the problem—it often is (*see below*).

2 Air cap is dirty If I haven't made a strong enough case for the importance of cleanliness in spray-painting so far, let me add this to the evidence. An air cap that's dirty or clogged can also cause sags and runs. This usually manifests itself in the form of sputtering, which lays down globs of finish that have no choice but to sag or run. You know the drill: Keep it clean.

3 Too close to the work surface Holding a spray gun too close to the surface is one of the most common causes of sags and runs. What you're basically doing here is applying too heavy a coat of finish.

Remember, you're always better off spraying on multiple, lighter coats than one heavy one. The general recommended distance for spraying is 8" to 12" from the surface.

4 **Not releasing trigger at end of stroke** In addition to causing overspray, not releasing the trigger at the end of a stroke can also result in sags and runs. Much of this depends on how fast you're moving the gun.

If you're going too slow, you could easily spray too much material onto the edges of the workpiece. Concentrate on releasing the trigger about 6" after the tip of the gun has passed the edge, and check to make sure that your stroke is fast enough; *see below.*

5 **Wrong angle to surface** Sags or runs can also be produced when the spray gun is held at a wrong angle to the work surface. At all times, the body of the spray gun should be held so it's parallel to the surface.

If it's not parallel, an uneven spray pattern will apply too heavy a coat on either the top or bottom, resulting in a finish that sags or runs.

6 **Too slow a stroke** Even if your gun is held the proper distance from the work surface and it's parallel, developing runs or sags is easy if your stroke is too slow. Keeping the gun moving at a good clip will prevent you from applying too heavy a coat.

As a general rule of thumb, I try to cover about a foot in a second. It's always easier to spray on another light coat than it is to deal with sags or runs.

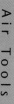

NAILER:
CROOKED FASTENERS

1 Problem Fasteners that go in crooked can create a disaster, especially if it's a finish piece of work like a piece of furniture. Basically, the fastener is deflected or "follows" the growth rings of the wood.

The first time I experienced this, I almost sat down and cried. I was pinning a plywood back onto a bookcase with my spiffy new brad nailer. I was so pleased at how easy it was, I didn't notice that virtually every brad I had shot had deflected and was now sticking out of the side of the bookcase. This was a painful way to learn not to shoot long, light-gauge brads into dense hardwood.

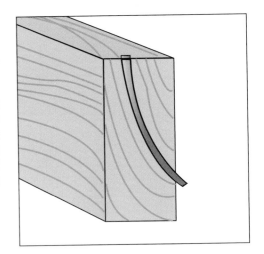

2 Follow the grain One solution to preventing crooked fasteners is to not fight city hall. That is, be aware of the grain and try to shoot fasteners with it, instead of against it. You can't always do this, and in those cases, try stepping up to a heavier-gauge fastener if possible.

If all else fails, you can do what cabinetmakers have done for years when nailing into hardwood: Drill a pilot hole and use a standard nail and (gasp!) a hammer.

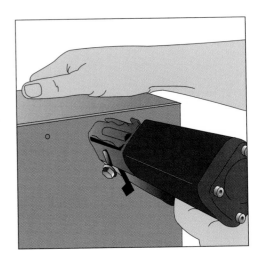

3 Change the angle Another way to help prevent fasteners from going in crooked due to dense grain is to change the angle of attack. Try tilting the gun to follow the grain or shoot directly perpendicular through it—whichever way you can to prevent the grain from steering or deflecting the fastener.

Just make sure that the material is thick enough that the fastener doesn't poke out through its face, and that your hands are clear of the work area.

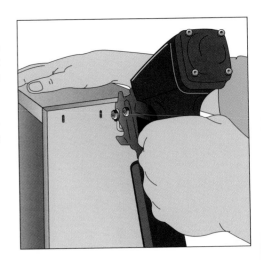

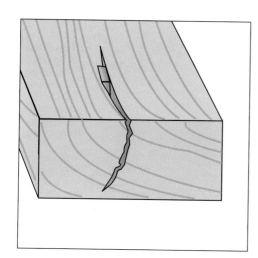

1 Problem Since air-driven fasteners are driven in a single shot, you're much less likely to experience splitting in wood than when using a hammer. But that's not to say that it doesn't happen. Splitting most often occurs near the edge of a workpiece or in thin, unsupported materials, like moldings.

In some cases, this is caused by simply using too large of a fastener. But most of the time it has to do with where you're nailing and how (*see below*).

2 Keep nose in from edge To prevent splitting in hardwood or softwood, it's best to keep the nosepiece of the nailer in from the edge whenever possible. Basically what you're doing here is providing as much support to the area around the fastener as possible. The closer you move toward the edge, the fewer wood fibers there are to support each other and prevent a split from occuring.

3 Orient the staple differently Since you're driving two points into the wood at the same time with a staple, you're more likely to cause a split than if you had used a nail or brad. Many times you can prevent this from happening by simply orienting the staple differently, as shown.

NAILER: SHOOTS MULTIPLE FASTENERS

1 Problem There are two problems that can arise when a nailer shoots multiple fasteners. First, if you're applying trim or molding that's in plain view, you'll end up with twice the indentation to cover up with wood putty. This might not seem like a big deal, but it can be when you've got a whole room worth of trim to put up. Second, multiple fasteners, especially when shot near an edge, can cause wood to split (*see page 123*).

2 Too slow a trigger pull Oddly enough, pulling a trigger too slowly, especially on finish nailers and brad nailers, can cause an air nailer to shoot more than one fastener at a time. The solution to this is simple. Once you position the nailer and press the nosepiece into the workpiece to engage the safety device, pull the trigger with authority.

3 Improper fasteners The most common reason I've seen for a nailer to shoot multiple fasteners is that the wrong fasteners are being used. Of course, air-nail manufacturers always recommend that you use their brand of fastener.

The important thing is to make sure to use the correct *type*. Check the body of the nailer (*as shown*) or the owner's manual to determine the correct fastener for the gun.

1 Problem A finish or brad nailer that leaves an indentation wherever it shoots a fastener can really ruin your day. The most common culprit here is the tip; *see below.* Another cause can be attributed how the trigger is pulled and also the recoil of the gun.

Whichever is the case, the problem can be solved. If you've noticed this after a job is done, either pull out a can of putty or, in some cases, you can steam out the dent by pressing a hot iron on a damp rag placed over the dent.

2 Use a rubber no-mar tip If your air nailer comes with a rubber no-mar tip like the one shown, you shouldn't be experiencing any denting.

If you do, carefully inspect the tip to make sure it's not worn and that it doesn't have a bit of metal or other hard substance embedded in the soft plastic. It's a good idea to keep an extra rubber tip on hand for situations like this.

3 Trigger release Air nailers with bent metal "no-mar" tips often cause dents in the wood when the trigger is pulled too slowly. Basically what happens is that the piston recoil at the end of the cycle causes the tip of the nailer to chatter, thereby denting the wood. The solution is a firm grip on the nailer, combined with a decisive pull of the trigger.

GLOSSARY

Air cap – a removable cap at the tip of a spray gun that atomizes fluid by directing compressed air into the fluid stream.

Air filter – a device, usually felt or foam, that separates and removes dust from air before it enters a compressor.

Air hose – a flexible plastic or rubber hose rated to handle compressed air. Air hose commonly comes in 25-, 50-, and 100-foot lengths.

Air nailer – any air-powered tool that shoots fasteners into a workpiece. When it's activated, compressed air forces a piston with an attached driver blade to drive the next fastener.

Air tank – a metal tank attached to a compressor to store air. Common types are pancake, cylindrical, and twin. Capacities range from 4 gallons to over 60.

Atomization – the process where compressed air breaks up fluid into tiny particles.

Bleeder gun – any spray gun that has air continuously moving through the tip of the gun.

Blush – a milky white cloud under a finish caused by trapped moisture.

Brad nailer – a type of nailer that's designed to shoot typically 18-gauge brads that can vary in length from ⅜" to 1½".

CFM (cubic feet per minute) – the volume of air being delivered by a compressor to an air tool, used as a measure of the compressor's capability; the actual amount of free air in cubic feet that a compressor can pump in one minute at working pressure.

Compressed air – free air that has been pressed into a volume smaller than it normally occupies. As compressed air exerts pressure, it performs work when released and allowed to expand to its normal free state.

Compressor – a machine designed for compressing air from an initial intake pressure to a higher discharge pressure.

Cup – a holder or material canister that attaches to a spray gun and stores finish to be sprayed.

Dryer – a type of filter that's attached to the air lines in a compressed air system that removes moisture, typically using chemical desiccants.

External-mix air cap – an air cap that mixes air into the fluid after it leaves the tip of the gun.

Finish nailer – a type of air nailer that shoots 15- and 16-gauge nails varying in length from ¾" to 2¾".

Framing nailer – a type of air nailer that shoots 6d to 16d (2" to 3¼" long) nails. Framing nailers are further defined by the type of magazine they use to hold fasteners, either coil or straight.

Gravity-feed – a type of spray gun where the material cup attaches above the gun. Material is forced into the gun via gravity.

Horns – a pair of holes that project from the perimeter of an external-mix air cap, used to control the pattern of the material being sprayed.

In-line filter – a device used to remove dirt, dust, and moisture from an air line. The most common type uses a whirlpool effect to trap contaminants as they flow through a chamber. Mechanical filters pass air through an absorbing material, usually in the form of a cartridge.

In-line sander – a type of sander that uses a back and forth motion that most approximates hand sanding. Often referred to as a straight-line sander, it uses long strips of sandpaper (typically 9" to 17") that are held in place with built-in clamps.

Internal-mix air cap – a type of air cap where the fluid mixes with the air inside the cap before being forced through a single opening.

Jitterbug sander – a type of sander (also referred to as an orbital sander) that moves the sanding pad in tiny orbits. It's not as aggressive as a random-orbit sander and is easier to use in confined spaces: The square pad allows you to reach into corners.

Lubricator – a lubricator (or oiler) is placed between the compressor and the air line to periodically inject tiny droplets of oil in the line to automatically lubricate air tools; should never be used with spray equipment, since the oil can contaminate the finish.

Nonbleeder gun – a type of spray gun that contains an internal valve that shuts off air to the gun when the trigger is released.

Oil-less compressor – a type of compressor that uses nonmetal piston rings and Teflon-coated parts in lieu of oil to keep things running smoothly.

Oil-lubricated compressor – a type of compressor that uses oil to lubricate the internal parts; consists of an air pump powered by either a gas engine or an electric motor, and a tank to store the compressed air.

Overspray – sprayed material that misses the target completely.

Petcock – a hand-operated device used to allow condensed moisture to drain out of the tank of a compressor.

Pinholes – small bubbles that appear in the surface of a dried finish, typically caused by material trapped in the pores of open-grained wood.

Portable compressor – any compressor that features a compressor and motor so mounted that they may be easily moved as a unit.

Pressure-feed – a type of spray system that uses a fluid cup or material tanks to move fluid to the tip of the spray gun.

PSI (pounds per square inch) – the measure of air pressure or force delivered to an air tool by the compressor.

Quick-connect fittings – special hose fittings that let you connect and disconnect tools from the air line without having to shut down the compressor; the female half of the male-female coupling pair has a built-in shut-off valve.

Random-orbit sander – a type of sander that's a hybrid of a disk sander and an orbital sander; it combines the large swirling motions of a disk sander with the smaller orbits of a jitterbug (orbital) sander.

Regulator – a device installed between a compressor and an air tool to control the pressure going to the tool. Most models have a built-in gauge to monitor outgoing pressure and provide a regulated output from 0 to 150 psi.

Relief valve – a safety device that will open to drain off excessive pressure that has built up in a tank; similar to the pressure-relief valve on a water heater.

SCFM (standard cubic feet per minute) – a cfm rating corrected for a given barometric pressure and temperature.

Sequential-trip – air nailers with sequential-trip firing systems require you to pull the trigger each time you want to shoot a fastener once the safety mechanism has been engaged.

Single-stage compressor – a type of compressor where compression from the initial to final pressure occurs in a single step or stage.

Siphon- (suction-) feed – a type of spray system that moves fluid into the atomizing air stream by creating a vacuum at the tip of the spray gun.

Spray gun – an air-powered tool that atomizes fluid by injecting compressed air into the fluid stream; it can be gravity-feed, pressure-feed, or siphon-feed.

Touch-trip – commonly referred to as "bounce" firing, this system allows you to hold the trigger down and shoot a fastener every time the contact point or safety mechanism is depressed.

Two-stage compressor – a compressor where the compression from the initial to final pressure is completed in two distinct steps or stages. After air is compressed in the first stage, it is passed to the second stage to be compressed further.

Viscosity – the measure of a fluid's thickness based on the internal molecular friction of the liquid.

Viscosity cup – a testing device that identifies a fluid's viscosity by timing how long it takes for the filled cup to empty via a small hole in its bottom.

INDEX